No Children.
It Makes Sense!

Nathalie Six

No children.
It Makes Sense!

Survey on the Phenomenon of Non-Parents

Max Milo

Max Milo Editions, Paris, 2023
www.maxmilo.com
ISBN : 978-2-31501-151-3

To the women in my life.

Foreword

Deconditioning

There are those who want it and those who don't. Are you, who are reading these lines, part of the pro- or the anti-? If you were attracted by this book, it is very likely that you do not have children, and *even more likely* that you do not want them. Don't worry, you're right! In this book, you will find arguments in your favor; the testimonies that you will discover will perhaps echo personal experiences, lived pains, reflections often heard and stigmatizations too often incurred. The women and men I have interviewed, about forty, have lifted a modest veil and opened their hearts to a situation that is still taboo. They belong to the 5% of the population who have chosen not to have children. This is called voluntary infertility (as opposed to involuntary infertility, which includes all couples who do not succeed in having a child, whether they are infertile or not).

Nevertheless, I hope that among my readers will also be many parents and future parents, because this book is largely dedicated to them. They too are right! Choosing to give life deserves just as much esteem and respect as preferring not to give it, which can bring suffering. The human race would become extinct in a little less than a century if all the people on this planet decided not to procreate. Childbearing, as we will see in the first chapter, is as much an innate as an acquired reflex. Nature pushes us to conceive children, but also our culture. What are the main arguments of the pronatalists? To have a child, they say, is the most wonderful proof of love, the realization of a common project, the quintessence of any couple in love; it is also to believe in the future, to leave a trace of oneself, to give a meaning to one's life... to fill a void, the anti-natalists will retort. The arguments of some are the honey of others, each one trying to demonstrate the incoherence of the reasoning of the opposite party and to dismantle their remarks. The question is not who is right and who is wrong, but who shows more bad faith. Contradictory? The subject is deeply subjective: the controversy between the anti- and the proponents cannot be summarized in a series of reasons so abruptly stated.

If the road to hell is paved with good intentions, then no doubt children are a wonderful example. To perpetuate oneself: the intention is commendable, but is it reasonable? Faced with the return in force of family values and the omnipresent, even omnipotent, model of the child king, sauve qui peut! A reflection posing the alternative is necessary to all, whether one wants to become a mother and father or not.

While France is the good pupil of Europe as regards the birth rate, why do women and men not feel the desire to have children? In this pronatalist environment, how do they live their difference? Their path off the beaten track, beyond the norm, intrigued me enough to make me want to dig deeper and investigate this minority that is often put on the back burner. At the same time, the book is also an opportunity to ask ourselves to what extent we can be influenced in our life choices, and if there is a place for self-fulfillment and self-realization without going through motherhood.

In reporting what people have said, I wanted to give a platform to "non-parents", barbarously and not very casually called "nulliparous". The term, adopted by sociologists, ethnologists, scientists and the medical profession in general, is already not very nice. The idea of nul(le), i.e. zero, is established when it is said: "which is equivalent to nothing"; very quickly, the word defines someone who would be empty, uninteresting, crazy, moody, complexed, psychotic, depressive. The amalgam is quickly made and caricatures abound. How are they observed, gauged, judged by the rest of society? Are they understood, rejected, or on the contrary jealous and secretly admired?

To answer this question, I went to interview them, and especially to listen to them. Similar to each other, or on the contrary totally opposed, younger or much older than me, they spoke to me about their only common point : being neither a mother, nor a father. I wanted to include men's testimonies, because I felt it was important to repair an injustice that is done to them in the majority of books dealing with this subject by excluding them. Whether they do not want children themselves or whether they are the husbands and partners of women who have made this choice, their place in this investigation seemed obvious to me. What are the reasons that push a man to refuse the role of father? What are the solutions available to them to make sure they never procreate? Conversely, when one loves a woman who has no desire for a child, what are the options? Finally, do a man and a woman accept equally and as easily to draw a line under a child to please their partner?

Among the "childless" there are many families: there are the passionate and exclusive lovers, the victims of psychological dramas or violence, the survivors of childhood, the artists, the careerists, the religious, the eternal children, the disappointed in life, the ecologists, the convinced Malthusians... Among the women, I also met activists (often feminists, but not always), those who have made their refusal to give birth into a standard, brandishing this absence of motherhood to assert themselves in a society that praises all mothers and family values. Then there are the discreet ones who, without saying anything or claiming anything, have voluntarily let the years pass when they "could" have become mothers, carefully avoiding the spotlight on them, dodging confrontations with the followers of motherhood. For a silent majority of them, it is a matter of diplomatically and smoothly bypassing the incessant question: "And you, when is it going to happen?"

Finally, the question is asked among both homosexuals and heterosexuals.

The writing of this book was both a quest and an investigation. During the interviews that were necessary for its elaboration, I tried never to judge my interlocutors. The questions I asked them were not intended to relieve or feed an unhealthy curiosity, but to try to understand their approach and their life choices. By confiding in me, sometimes with difficulty and awkwardness, or on the contrary with generosity and an extreme lucidity about themselves, these women and men have shown me confidence and have pushed me to my limits, forcing me to face up to disturbing theses that I did not want to consider.

This book is an adventure. First, because I wanted to answer several politically incorrect questions, and second, because I wanted to be personally involved in this investigation. When I started writing it, I was about to turn 30. What do you think a 30-year-old girl thinks about? About getting married, about having a child? Is she really thinking about it, sincerely, freely, or is it society that thinks about it for her? The goal was to know if it is possible to free oneself from an education, from a cultural and social heritage, from a family tradition, and to distinguish oneself from one's friends and professional environment. When a couple chooses to have a child, are they alone in this choice? Who accompanies them in spite of their decision? In a word, are we really free to decide?

Since my late teens, I felt the obligation that I would have to become a mother one day. Where did this feeling take root? Was it even conscious? However, from the moment I started earning a living, the desire to have children, without disappearing entirely, was relegated to the rank of a distant project. Becoming a parent, yes, but not right away. When then? More and more people in their thirties don't know how to answer this question. In this category, we are not only talking about "single women", Don Juan, but also about married couples, civil partnerships or simply cohabiting couples who put off until the Greek calendars the moment to create a home.

Feeling that I would surely become a mother one day, I wanted to at least know why. Not to have a child by chance. To be the reasoned object of my own desire.

For the others, parents, future parents, those who are reluctant to parent in some or all of its forms, the question deserves to be asked. So that each and everyone feels good about the path he or she has chosen to take.

Chapter 1

Do we really know why we have children?

The weight of the collective unconscious

Before listing all the reasons that push women and men not to have children, it would be good to ask ourselves why the majority of the inhabitants of the planet do.

Having children is an act that seems to many people to be natural, the result of a historical, cultural and social movement, so much so that the question: "Why do we want children?" seems (almost) superfluous. However, it is not useless to ask the question. Our era has gone from the verb "to have" children to the verb "to make" children, with the important step of "wanting" children. Why? Quite simply, because before, until the 1960s, procreation was difficult to control, the institution of marriage and the union of the sexes resulting in the vast majority of cases in the birth of one or more children. The child would thus be a gift that cannot be refused or questioned. To attack this postulate is to defy the more or less conscious prohibition that is attached to it by discussing it. To pose the alternative is revolutionary. After centuries of social and cultural conformism, it is possible to ask ourselves if we want to be parents.

"It would be one of the greatest triumphs of mankind [...] if the responsible act of procreation could be raised to the level of a voluntary and intentional action[1]", wrote Sigmund Freud. Today, the dream of the inventor of psychoanalysis is within reach: control of fertilization via the condom, the pill and the IUD, etc. In spite of these medical advances and the scientific prowess to come, conceiving a child is still most often the result of a set of factors that go far beyond the private sphere. Traditionally, a woman has children to conform to a collective unconscious that aims at the reproduction of the species. She desires children because she wants to belong to a group. Need for recognition by society and the family circle, desire for omnipotence through her child, narcissistic aspiration and mirror effect, desire for a fusional link often unavailable in the couple, desire to give love, fantasy child. What is the conscious and unconscious part in this decision (when there is a decision, which is far from being the case for all couples)?

---

1. The exact phrase is: "It would theoretically be one of the greatest triumphs of humanity, one of the most tangible liberations from the natural constraint to which our species is subjected, if we succeeded in raising the responsible act of procreation to the rank of a voluntary and intentional action, and in freeing it from its entanglement with the necessary satisfaction of a natural need." *In Sexuality in the Etiology of Neuroses.* Cf. *La Première Théorie des névroses,* Presses universitaires de France, collection Quadrige, p. 172.

According to a survey carried out by TNS-Sofres for *Philosophie magazine*[2], 73% of the people questioned have children for "pleasure", 69% for "duty" and 48% for "love". Obviously, one answer does not exclude the others; several motivations can preside over the desire to have children. The aim was to identify the dominant principle.

By "pleasure", the interviewees mean that a child "makes everyday life more beautiful, more joyful, that it is a new experience that introduces novelty, that a child allows one to leave a part of oneself on Earth after one's death and that through him, one can achieve what one could not do oneself". By "duty", the interviewees mean "to keep one's family alive, to transmit one's values, one's history, to give the gift of life to someone, to become an adult, to take responsibility, to have a child to fulfill one's partner's wish, by religious or ethical choice". By "love", they consider that a child "gives affection, love and allows to be less lonely when one gets older, and makes the couple relationship more intense and solid". This study is of particular interest to us here because it points out reasons that will be found with a mirror effect among people who do not want children. Thus, the question of the couple appears to be very important for both of them. In view of this survey and the testimonies collected, the question is not

---

2. "Why do we have children?", *Philosophy magazine*, March 2009, n° 27. The survey was conducted from January 2 to 5, 2009 on a sample of 1,000 people representative of the entire population aged 18 and over, according to the quota method. The total number of responses is greater than 100, as respondents may have given several answers.

Do we really know why we have children?

clear-cut as to whether a child disrupts and sabotages the life of the couple, or on the contrary, whether it is an enriching and positive element. Perhaps a little of both?

Fourth and last category of arguments, the ontological reason (study of the being as being) borrowed from the philosopher Emmanuel Levinas who provides a daring explanation of fatherhood and motherhood. For him, having a child allows one to come out of oneself, to extend oneself, not to be a prisoner of one's identity, insofar as the child is at the same time "radically other" and in some way, a "mini me". One would find his metaphysical plenitude only through his child. This last point remains as much to be questioned as the previous ones. The idea that the fulfillment of the being passes by a third person and is revealed in contact with another self which is at the same time an independent person is obviously not shared by all. By oversimplifying it, this vision of parenthood seems dangerous, because it could lead to the creation of categories: are some parents more so than others? *What about* adopted children, those conceived by artificial insemination, with egg and sperm donation, or via a surrogate mother? Is this ontological role still applicable to this kind of fatherhood and motherhood? On the contrary, history shows that filiation is often a symbolic construction, where genes are not the determining element. In married couples, the father is the husband of the mother, and in unmarried couples, the father is the one who designates himself as such. Will DNA testing, which is increasingly practiced, undermine this data? There is no doubt that this trend will also have consequences on the notion of parenthood.

Let's come back to the question of "duty", obviously important in the choice of parenthood, in addition to that of pleasure. Childbirth is not only the result of religious pressure, it does not only concern bigots, believers and churchgoers, it is also social, ethical and metaphysical.

The social duty is explained by the heteronomy, i.e. the incapacity of the individual to found himself his own laws, which is then satisfied to conform to an external rule. This submission will take the appearance of a simple academism or, more serious, of a total alienation. Some couples literally force themselves to procreate for fear of facing the gaze of society, the family, religious authorities, and of being summoned to explain their refusal. Rare are those, being parents, who admit *a posteriori* having had children by social conformity. It is easier and more comfortable to invent reasons linked to love, to joy and to talk about maternal instinct.

From a spiritual point of view, we have children to return the gift we were given at birth; we respond to the gift of life with the gift of life. Obviously, there is no contract or rule that obliges human beings to pay tribute to the community in this way. The other side of this equation, more pragmatic this time, would be to give a gift to those who gave birth to us, that is, our own parents. There is no doubt that children are not a repayment, even if it often turns out in practice that the arrival of grandchildren is a real joy for the previous generations. How many show themselves to be better in their role as grandparents than as parents? Can we then see this as a reparation, or is this vision of things abusive and does it constitute an *a posteriori* demonstration?

We will see throughout the book that the notions of duty, as well as those of pleasure, hedonism and egoism, potentially belong to both camps: the pronatalists and the anti-natalists. Selfishness, in particular, an argument often used as a weapon against the "childless", also applies to many parents: one can have a child to make one's life more joyful, to create a "hybrid" being that embodies the union of two people who love each other, to have at one's disposal a little loving companion, a source of sweetness and dependence on one's self, in order to feel one's existence. The desire for a child is rarely disinterested. In spite of everything, an irrepressible reason seems to top the edifice, as Marcel Gauchet concludes, who was interested in the question in "L'enfant du désir"[3]. For him, procreation is linked "to the forces of life in which our animality participates". Biologically, we continue to reproduce, like all the other mammals, to perpetuate our species, animated by an irrational vital impulse. From there to conclude that women and men who do not wish to have children are not animated by such a drive, there is only one step.

However, the reality is more complex than that. First, because we cannot ignore the environment and the context in which these women and men make their decisions. At the

---

3. "L'enfant du désir", *Le Débat* n° 132, November-December 2004, *Philosophie magazine* n° 27, March 2009.

beginning of the 21st century, we cannot say that the human species is in danger and that there is a risk of extinction. With its 6.8 billion human beings, our planet is rather over-populated than the opposite. This is one of the arguments put forward by the "childless"[4]. Secondly, some women and men may have succeeded in taming their vital impulse; this is the case of those who live in abstinence, especially religious people, whose choice is guided by a spiritual commitment[5], it is also the case of people who feel that they do not have sufficient financial means to raise a child and prefer to curb their fleeting desire[6]; women and men whose childhood was so badly treated that they are psychically unable to reproduce and to let this vital impulse speak. These people must first heal the suffering child within them before being able to project themselves into the future and identify themselves as potential parents[7]. Finally, by refusing to have children in order to preserve the Great Love, some couples kick Schopenhauer's philosophical argument to the curb when he writes that "the passion of love has in view only the procreation of an individual of a determined nature[8]" and that the exaltation of the lovers is only the echo of the "sighs of joy of the Genius of the species, when he succeeds in taking advantage of a unique opportunity to realize his projects[9]". Is love only an illusion,

---

4. See Chapter 7.
5. See Chapter 9.
6. See Chapter 8.
7. See Chapter 5.
8. *In* SCHOPENHAUER (Arthur), *The World as Will and as Representation.*
9. *Ibid.*

Do we really know why we have children?

a trick of nature to procreate? Not according to these couples who talk about their passion and their love links outside of any child project[10]. The individual impulse to preserve our genes, the desire for immortality of the species, is therefore not shared by all.

The refusal to procreate, the no kid: childfree or childless?

Finally, if procreating is rarely the result of a conscious choice because it is the norm - the majority of women give birth on earth and have done so for thousands of years without really thinking about it -, on the other hand, refusing to procreate forces us to reflect on ourselves and on the society around us. Why don't I want to have a child when everyone around me has one?

Whether it is made with full knowledge of the facts or generated by obscure reasons that it will be good to unravel and know, the refusal to give birth for a woman, the refusal to take on the role of father for a man, is absolutely not insignificant. It is a silent declaration, a decision sometimes heavy to bear, sometimes full of promise and freedom. An affirmation of oneself.

The term *"no kid"* is a banner under which "non-parents" from all countries gather. It appeared on the French editorial

---

10. See Chapter 3.

No Children. It Makes Sense!

scene with the publication of Corinne Maier's booklet *No Kid*[11], which gave readers "Forty reasons not to have children". Since then, the psychoanalyst, who is also the mother of two children, has been emulated. "Childfree" groups are flourishing on the Web, invading social networks like Facebook. The logo is always the same and the message is clear: "Hell is children". Whatever their country of origin, they generally agree on these five principles:

1. You have the right to choose not to have children;

2. You are equal to people who have children;

3. You are not being selfish by choosing not to have children and you should not be made to feel guilty for making this choice;

4. Happy childless *Big Kids* contribute or can contribute to society in ways other than reproduction;

5. Having children does not make them better, it makes them parents, good or bad.

The English language offers the advantage of being able to play with the word "freedom" in conjunction with the word "child": thus, *childless* and *childfree* do not have the same meaning at all, whereas their translation into French would be identical if we are not careful. *Childless* refers to all women and men who have to face an unchosen infertility (sterility, psychological infertility, absence of partner, refusal of partner, accident of life, etc.) while *childfree* defines individuals "who have chosen not to have any or who do not want

---

11. MAIER (Corinne), *No Kid. Forty reasons not to have children*, Michalon, Paris, 2003.

Do we really know why we have children?

any". Without children, they feel free, uninhibited, and enjoy what life has to offer thanks to their non-parental status. The former may see the absence of a child as a lack, a negative fact, while the latter fully appreciate their situation.

Having now specified these terms, I will take the liberty throughout this book of using them here and there so as not to weigh down my sentences too much by the equivalent which exists however in the language of Molière.

Chapter 2

Voluntary infertility

The way in which I conducted this survey is in itself indicative of the taboo that exists around not wanting a child. When I had to find people who would agree to tell me their experiences, I had to expressly mention that their testimonies would be anonymous. This was an unavoidable condition for the majority. "Putting a name to a testimony like that? You don't think about it," I was told almost every time. The women who agreed to speak openly could be counted on the fingers of one hand. Two of them insisted that I not change their names and that they be easily identifiable. In both cases, the writer Nathalie Rheims and the psychoanalyst Claude Schlienger, they are women in agreement with themselves, with an extremely coherent background, having thought long and hard about their place as women - women who have not experienced motherhood. I would even say more: they seemed serene to me. Strong heads, with strong characters, they are also women that life has not spared, having known and gone through ordeals, without leaving them drained or bitter, mean or depressed. This point seems to me important to underline, because the prevailing discourse wants to make the "childless" appear either as potential egoists, depressives and chronic pessimists, or, as far as women are concerned, as repressed lesbians, neurotic hysterics obsessed with their bodies. This does not mean that all those who do not want children are perfectly happy and balanced. Some, as we will see, are not happy with themselves, and hide behind their lack of desire for a child an absence of desire at all, others repress images of a damaged childhood. Others simply have professional and aesthetic priorities that do not go well with the arrival of a child. However, let's stop caricaturing these women and men and taking some particular cases as generalities.

From a sociological point of view, and not only a psychological one, the situation of couples has changed. As Arnaud Régnier-Loilier explains very well, with the introduction of contraception "couples have left the ranks of natural fertility and even directed fertility; they are now in a state of infertility. Infertility is the reversible state of couples who have no chance of conceiving during a normal cycle because they have protected their intercourse. The woman is now permanently unfertile, unless she voluntarily takes action to the contrary. Whereas couples used to have to intervene to make their sexual relations non-fertile, they now have to intervene before intercourse if they wish to procreate. The relationship that couples have with their fertility is therefore diametrically opposed[12]."

In France, remaining childless is more often a matter of choice, or induced by one's life course, than a determined and stable life choice over time[13]. In the course of his or her life, the same individual will also have to deal with the desire or lack of desire for children from potential spouses. In general, there is a strong feeling of infertility in our society, which is due to a pressure from society, rooted in cultural reflexes. Undoubtedly, the experience of parenthood is nowadays highly valued.

For most of us, the idea of motherhood is a legacy of our family heritage. Personally, children were part of my family, cultural and social codes. Everything has always encouraged me to have them, to hope for them, to desire them. Now, I am an adult and for the first time in my life, I am able to ask myself this question: do I really want to have children? Is it a matter of course, as I have been told since my first games as a little girl? Do I want to have them now, later, or never? What kind of life do I want to build? I hesitate between entering the mainstream or categorically deferring to it and taking a path that will not resemble that of my mother's generation (the *Wonder Women* who simultaneously assumed a large family and a career, sometimes to the detriment of family balance

---

12. *Avoir des enfants en France, désirs et réalité*, Ined éditions, p. 36.
13. Toulemon (Laurent), "Très peu de couples restent volontairement sans enfant", *Population*, n° 4-5, July-October 1995, p. 1079-1109.

or their health) or that of my grandmother (the generation of housewives who had no choice but to raise their children, to hold on to them at all costs, outside of any contraception and before the right to abortion).

Added to the cultural pressure in France is an ideal that knows no borders, emanating from the cinema, *showbiz* and the *jet set*, where actresses, singers and top models are constantly flaunting their maternity in the newspapers. As one of the women I interviewed remarked, "Political correctness pushes us to have babies. I am very struck by the image of *celebrities* (such as Angelina Jolie and Madonna) which adds to the general pressure. Even they, the canons of beauty and *fashion* icons, references of ready-to-think, they are involved!" Via the written press, television or the Internet, French women are showered with images of "modern" and attractive Madonnas. The mother who was once confined to the house to look after the children and the household, curlers on her head, permanently draped in a smudged apron and having no time to apply make-up, has been transformed under the spotlight into a superb model, with a rounded belly that disappears immediately after giving birth. In just a few days, the parturient is transformed into a wiry, tanned, smiling and muscular *bimbo*, with a child in each arm, dressed in the latest fashion and bursting with happiness and health. How can we fight against this model, which seems to be fundamentalist to some and which causes more anxiety to all women who do not want to have children or who have not succeeded in having any? Once they have decided to have a child, women, if they do not succeed, quickly feel a sense of failure (especially in environments where fertility is traditionally higher). Stopping their contraceptive method should be followed by an immediate effect, but this is often not the case. Nature needs time; our age has run out of time.

The French demographic situation of non-parenthood

The study of demography in France began well before the Second World War, but it was with the creation of INED (Institut national des études démographiques) in 1945 and then INSEE (Institut national de la statistique et des études économiques) in 1946 that it took on its modern dimension and that it finally had measurement tools worthy of the name and significant dedicated funding. One of the missions of INED and INSEE is to organize and conduct population censuses and general interest surveys (regular or ad hoc) of businesses and households. It is thanks to these two institutes that we can now measure what interests us here: the fertility intentions of the French population.

Curiously, among all the surveys and figures available for more than fifty years on the French population (birth rate, fertility rate, infant mortality rate, etc.), infertility is the bad pupil of the class, an almost forgotten element. This is certainly not by chance. Perhaps the subject has not interested anyone until now, or has been considered marginal to the point of being relegated to the rank of invisible minorities.

A new generation of demographers and sociologists seems to want to fill this gap and has been working on the issue for a few years: at INED, I met or spoke by phone with Laurent Toulemon[14], Magali Mazière and Charlotte Debest. The articles by Arnaud Régnier-Loilier[15], Ariane Pailhé and Anne Solaz[16] (Ined), Pascale Donati[17] (doctoral student in sociology at the University of Versailles-Saint-Quentin-en-Yvelines attached to the laboratory Printemps - Professions, institutions and temporalities), and Maria Rita Testa[18] (from the Institute of Demography in Vienna, Austria) have also enlightened me.

In general, infertility (voluntary or involuntary) is quite low in France (compared to other European countries). It is higher among men than among women and is quite socially polarized: men without children tend to be at the bottom

---

14. TOULEMON (Laurent), TESTA (Maria Rita), "Fécondité envisagée, fécondité réalisée : un lien complexe", *Population et Société*, n° 415, September 2005. The entire issue was written by these two sociologists on the theme of intended fertility and realized fertility.

15. *Portraits de familles*, under the direction of Arnaud Régnier-Loilier, éditions de l'Ined, collection Grandes enquêtes, 2009, 543 p.; *Avoir des enfants en France, Désirs et réalités*, preface by Henri Leridon, collection les Cahiers de l'Ined, éditions de l'Ined, 2007, 267 p.

16. PAILHÉ (Ariane) and SOLAZ (Anne), "Vie professionnelle et naissance : la charge de la conciliation repose essentiellement sur les femmes", *Population et Société*, Ined monthly newsletter, n° 426, September 2006.

17. DONATI (Pascale), "L'Absence d'enfants. Un choix plus ou moins délibéré dans le parcours d'hommes et de femmes", revue *Politiques sociales et familiales*, décembre 2000, p. 43-56.

18. TOULEMON (Laurent) and TESTA (Marita Rita), "Fécondité envisagée, fécondité réalisée : un lien complexe", *op. cit.*

of the social ladder, whereas women without children are more often at the top. The reason is both financial and socio-cultural. In order to feel fulfilled and to "exist", a woman who is a senior executive, married or not, has less need to raise children than a woman without a job and without diplomas. In disadvantaged areas in general, women find fulfillment and a place by becoming mothers. On the other hand, a man who is unemployed, and therefore has no income, and moreover has a low level of education, has a high probability of being excluded from the matrimonial market; he will therefore have great difficulty in starting a family.

As for women or couples who claim to remain childless, sociologists and demographers, again, agree that they know little. A research project targeting "voluntary infertility" began in 2009, led by a sociology student, Charlotte Debest, who is writing her thesis on the subject. To date, the most relevant work, from a quantitative point of view, is that of Laurent Toulemon[19] who has published an article on his results on the realization of fertility intentions[20]. What do we discover? That women who have remained childless "voluntarily" represent about 5% of all women, while couples who have never wanted a child and have not had one represent 4%. This infertility remains moderate compared to that of other European countries: Germany is in first place, followed by

---

19. TOULEMON (Laurent), "Très peu de couples restent volontairement sans enfant", *op. cit.* p. 1079-1109.
20. TOULEMON (Laurent) and TESTA (Marita Rita), "Fécondité envisagée, fécondité réalisée : un lien complexe", *op. cit.*

Voluntary infertility

Finland and England, while France is just before last, playing neck and neck with Poland.

Looking at intentions, those who said they did not want children did a fairly good job of carrying out their intentions (only 3 percent actually had children within five years[21]). Unfortunately, the survey confuses women and men who already have children and no longer want them with those who have never had children and do not want them. The difficulty of such a survey is intrinsically linked to its method: "Strictly speaking, men and women should be asked once about the number of children they wish to have over a given period (the next five years, for example) and then asked again at the end of the period to find out to what extent they have achieved their plans. This longitudinal method is more time-consuming and costly than the instantaneous approach and has rarely been used in France to date[22]." A survey was nevertheless conducted by INSEE at the request of INED between 1998 and 2003[23]. The results tell me that a margin of thirty-year-olds is like me, undecided on the subject. 29% of them expect to have a child within six months, and 28% think not. "But it's immediately to point out, in one out of three cases, that they may well, by then, change their minds." There is a lot of wiggle room and it opens up a lot of possible scenarios. The most common response seems to be a wait-and-see attitude.

---

21. *Id.* at 2.
22. *Id.* at 1.
23. Survey of 2,624 men and women aged 15-45, conducted at the request of INED in September 1998. *Id.* at 1 and 2. 2.

What is the influence of marriage
and cohabitation on non-parenthood?

Another point that emerges from this survey concerns me: if the percentage of people declaring that they do not want a child is higher among singles, it is the same among cohabitants and married couples. Thus, marriage cannot be considered a trigger. Couples who have not decided to take the plunge, even if they are married, may remain childless for several years before eventually changing their choice... no more and no less than "cohabitants." Among the 36 people whose testimonies I have collected, 11 are married or in a couple.

For Marie, 34 years old, who just got married a few months ago, neither her marriage nor her life as a couple are a first step before motherhood:

"My husband, Martin, didn't want children and still doesn't - I might add, even less since his own: he has two that he adores, from a previous union, but he was "tricked" by his former partner. This is also why we have found each other. We live a perfectly happy life, because we are free of family constraints. My other half works like crazy and I am a heavy sleeper. Our happiness is to go back to bed on Saturday morning after breakfast and then wake up usually around 1 pm. This is totally incompatible with having children to take care of. We also go out to the theater a lot, we entertain a lot. These are all activities that the children would take away from us, depriving us of our freedom and carefreeness. In my opinion, we don't have to submit to it, there is no way I'm going to give it up."

Another case is that of Jennifer, 38, who has been in a relationship for seven years with a man nine years younger than her. When she met him, she was already sure she didn't want a child. She had no expectations of Prince Charming to start a family. What to do when you fall in love with a young man who has every chance of wanting to become a father one day?

"When I met Johann, it was love at first sight. After a year, I felt that something was not right. Unconsciously, a subject remained in suspense and interfered between us, in a silent way since we had never mentioned it. I asked him to put his cards on the table and tell me what was wrong. He told me that he didn't want to have children and was afraid that I would end up asking him to have children anyway. Of course, I was delighted to hear this confession because it was completely in line with my own personal views. I confided in him and warned him that his judgment might change. As the years went by, it was likely that he would want to start a family, perhaps even persuade me to become a mother. I told him that I would find this normal, predictable, but that there was little chance that he would change my mind. Worse: what if he woke up when I was past childbearing age myself?"

After this discussion, Jennifer and Johann continued to love each other, their life as a couple grew, their love matured and their initial common position was strengthened. Johann even became more firm on the issue of children. But when a health problem interfered with this choice, Jennifer's concern returned:

"Two years ago, I was diagnosed with a fibroid[24]. It was benign, but I was concerned and immediately thought about surgery, and the possibility of infertility. At that point, I spoke to my boyfriend again and asked him if he knew what this meant for our relationship. If I became infertile and he wanted to have a child in a few years, what would happen? He replied that if one day (which he still doesn't believe) we wanted a child, and I couldn't give one to him, there were enough unhappy children to adopt to solve the problem."

Jennifer was reassured that the man she loved was more committed than ever and that if he changed his mind, he would prefer to adopt with her rather than have a child through natural means with another woman. In any case, Jennifer did not have to face this alternative, because shortly afterwards she treated her fibroid, which disappeared without having made her sterile. In the meantime, her couple was strengthened by this ordeal.

Two-thirds of the people I interviewed were single at the time of the interview and most had never been married. It is clear that being single or living alone is a negative factor on the desire for parenthood. Not having found the right partner is a very good reason for not having children. This

---

24. A benign tumor developed from the uterine muscle, also called myometrium, and the fibrous tissue of the uterus.

is, for example, the point of view of Suzanne, a secretary in an international tax law firm, who sums up quite well what I have often heard:

"I didn't meet the man I was waiting for or who would have made me want to have a child. In my eyes, it's a couple's project, I never considered, as some women do, at the age of 40, to have a child alone. I find that very selfish."

As another of my speakers, Laurène, rightly pointed out, "from a biological point of view, it is very easy to have a child, and it will become easier and easier with medical manipulations and reproductive aids (*in vitro* fertilization). However, for me, having a child seems to be the project of a couple who love each other. Unfortunately, I observe that an individualistic machine has been set in motion. We need a child to perfect the panoply of the brilliant and modern young woman."

Personally, I am interested in this "panoply" because it determines the modern diktats that we are subjected to and that we impose on ourselves. The list is long of conscious and unconscious "duties" that build our lives. They also generate a host of moral and social prejudices. Among these, motherhood and parenthood have a special place. Omnipotent. Thus, each age undergoes its trial of intention, which swells with each additional ten...

20 years: the age of unreason

A teenager, *especially* a teenage girl, who declares that he or she does not want to have children, will be told most of the time: "You are so young, it is normal that you do not think about motherhood, you will see that it will come when you are older."

For this book, I must admit that I favored the testimonies of volunteers over 30 years old. Nevertheless, I gave the floor to Olivia, who is only 21 years old, because her claims seemed to me particularly strong and sincere. Moreover, as a student in nursing school, she has a background in working with children and babies. More than any other woman her age, she is in a position to appreciate what it means to have a child from a medical point of view. When I spoke with her, the question that kept coming up was the one that everyone, family and friends, kept asking her about: her youth.

"Everyone keeps bugging me that I don't know what I'm talking about and that I'm bound to change my mind. No one takes me seriously because I'm only 21, but I can assure you that I've already thought about it. Children are a nuisance, once they are there you can't give them back and there is no way to prevent them from being ungrateful, from having problems that you have to deal with. I don't want that responsibility. Besides, I don't feel any attraction as a woman for the little ones. I don't have a maternal streak."

This feeling could still evolve, I point out to him.

"Not a chance, because that's just one reason among many. I've thought about it a lot. I don't want to be burdened with offspring, it's a pattern that I never wanted, when I was a little girl already, I knew that I wouldn't have children later on! I don't want children and I can assure you that I won't have any."

Are you willing to take the bet that I will ask her again in 5, 10 or 15 years?

"Absolutely, you can check it out."

30 years: suspicion and questions from family and friends

Until I was 29 and a half, the milestone of 30 was never a topic of conversation per se, rather a good exercise in letting my mockery run free. "So what about 30?" I used to alternate between exasperation and indifference toward those who felt threatened, upset by this deadline. I used to ask myself: can a number really make a difference in a life? Why should I feel unease, urgency, the imminence of a struggle, at the advent of my thirtieth year? Having lived through the experience recently, the phenomenon leaves me perplexed. I have to admit that it is not so insignificant.

The second thing that puzzles me is why I associate my thirties with motherhood. Is the equation obvious for everyone or does it appear that way to me alone? The same challenge haunts me in both cases: if 7 is the age of reason, at what age do we become adults?

Does changing ten years, entering a new decade, make you grow up to the point of being able to pass on your knowledge, to guide a younger person? We have the folly, or the wisdom, to believe that if maturity is not measured by the number of years, the passage of time is likely to make us more mature. Unfortunately, the course of history proves to us that there is no truth in this field and that men do not improve according to an exact law. It would be too simple!

A child now? I wish I didn't have to choose: stop taking the pill or continue to be protected. Over time, that word "protect" changes its meaning. Does the pill protect or imprison? I'm not sure I always use the same word over time. This liberation of women is also an impediment to going in circles; it spoils everything, the surprise, the unexpected and the spontaneity, the impulse of a heart towards another on a summer night. A child as a birthday present, a folly that one assumes; everything but an event marked in red ink in one's agenda, after having written the wedding. Because one must first get married, it seems.

I began to feel a change in the questions that were or were not dared to ask me. Strangely enough, the evolution took place in a lightning and sudden way. It was as if the number "30" had signaled the beginning of a new era. I leave behind, forced and obliged, my twenties, that is to say the end of my adolescence, the blessed period when I was a student and then a young woman entering the active life. If I left the family nest at the age of 19, I only really took off and distanced myself, at least financially, from my family at the age of 23. First salary, first studio paid by me. I was thus able to cut the umbilical cord, to definitively leave the stage of childhood, while not yet entering the circle of the adults. How to name this state where one is still very young in his head, in his life habits, in his culture, but where one has nevertheless acquired real responsibilities? Some sociologists have found a term, "the adulescents" to designate these adult babies, or this group of adolescents who have long since come of age. I suddenly found myself in full possession of my rights on a par with my duties. In my eyes, parents had more duties than rights. I had no desire to know this right away. My case is not exceptional, it is similar to that of many teenagers who become students before entering the job market.

Until I was 29, life seemed interchangeable. I had before my eyes a range of choices as vast as the horizon. I could decide to change jobs, to move, to leave my country, to discover other spheres while telling myself that I was a beginner, that I was learning life. Everything would be beneficial and useful to me, enriching my main material: myself. Many of us think this, act on this belief that we are constantly given a second chance as long as we are protected by the bar of our twenties. How can we explain that so many young adults around their thirties start their studies again, sometimes from scratch? Bathed in the medical faith that we will be young for longer and longer, we end up believing in it like a rock. The shock came from others, by others. From my thirtieth year onwards, people close to me and (oh surprise!) people who were not close to me at all, began to ask me very personal questions about my intentions for motherhood. Did I intend to have a child soon? How many children would I like to have?

Sometimes it went as far as much more intimate questions, "Are you off the pill?" with the *ultimate in* my eyes being this unflinchingly pragmatic question, "When are you planning your first child?"

It is strange, even now when I think back, to notice the difference in attitudes of my entourage between my twenty-ninth and my thirtieth year. A few months that, physically, did not change me at all, but that nevertheless generated a new posture in some people. Another anecdote, that of Jennifer, is typical of what happens to many young women at this age:

"The first time someone made me feel like not being a mom was weird, I was 30. I was out at a club with a friend and we got hit on. As the conversation went on, one of the two guys asked me how old I was and if I had children. When I told him no, he didn't believe me. He exclaimed that it wasn't possible. Imagine his face when I told him that it wasn't certain that I would ever have children. In his eyes, I was not a "normal" girl. I told him that I was *only* 30 years old anyway, so so far there was nothing unusual or catastrophic. I was dumbfounded. I thought maybe I should reconsider. But no, actually, I think he was more the abnormal one."

Would it have been the same for a man? Would men be safer from suspicion and accusations than women? At first I thought so, but the testimonies I received do not all point in the same direction.

Around the age of 30, a man will *generally* not attract any anxious look from his entourage who will see in him, at worst a hardened bachelor, at best an eternal adolescent, likely to evolve very quickly. I write *generally*, because as in grammar, the exception confirms the rule. There are families where parents and children, even when they are grown up, do not dare to talk to each other: this lack of communication can easily lead to misunderstandings. Imagine a young adult who never brings home a girlfriend. This lack of commitment, especially if it is accompanied by a discourse of the type: "Let's be clear, I will never have children!" can make parents believe that their son is homosexual, another taboo still alive in our so-called modern society. Why not discuss it in these cases? What prevents parents from asking their child the question straightforwardly? Is it excessive modesty or the fear of having a different or even "deviant" offspring[25]? Faced with taboos and fears, tongues freeze. A wall of silence rises up between them, generating misunderstanding and then establishing distance.

As for reassuring oneself that one's son "remains an eternal teenager", this can be smiling or, on the contrary, appear very humiliating. It is not because one is a 30 year old man that one is not capable of having a clear, clear-cut and mature opinion on one's destiny. Christophe has thus very badly received the attitude of his parents towards him.

"It is not easy to make people around me understand this choice. The biggest lack of respect seems to come from my parents who think that at 30 years old, this choice is only a

---

25. In Durkheim's sociological sense, deviance is defined as a departure from the norm. This term obviously does not imply any value judgment.

dream of a retarded kid and that I will be irrevocably brought to change.

Recently, one of my cousins, who is two years older than me and already has two daughters, said at a family gathering, "Sometimes the ones who are late catch up with us!" with a knowing look on his face, as if he was holding out a pole to save my face.

Obviously, I don't think I'm especially behind him... Maybe even a little ahead of him, given that I have the freedom he'll only regain in his 50s..."

On the eve of his thirtieth birthday, Victor has no desire to have a child. He says he has no doubt about it. This choice was however put to the test, because it was the main reason for his breakup with his partner, after six years of relationship. Understanding that she would not make him change his mind, she preferred to leave. Contrary to Christophe, around him, nobody thought of reproaching him.

"Having or not having children is a subject that comes up from time to time between friends. I don't have a problem with the fact that I don't want any, my friends don't judge me. It's a fairly recent topic of conversation, I didn't think about it at all when I was 20."

Before breaking up, the question had become heavy between his girlfriend and him:

"There was no point in arguing, I didn't need to hear his arguments, I didn't want to, period. We didn't have the same *timing*. In the end, it became unhealthy, I was afraid she was pregnant. If she had been, I couldn't imagine keeping the child for a second, so yes, I did think about abortion. Since then, the question has not arisen with another girl, because I avoid long stories. I want to travel."

Thus, not only does Victor have absolutely no regrets, but he protects himself from having to face such a dilemma again. A woman could just as easily adopt the same attitude. However, wouldn't she receive more or less strong pressure from her entourage to change her mind? Victor has never felt a single accusing look towards him.

"My parents leave me alone with fatherhood, they don't interfere with my personal life, they don't try to influence me."

Stanislas, a lawyer in Nice, also had no trouble getting his choice accepted. At 32, he had already informed his father and stepmother (his father remarried after his wife's death) that he did not want to start a family and that his father would probably not have any grandchildren other than those his sister had given him.

"They get it, they leave me alone, I'm not pressured."

In addition to his lifestyle, which gives priority to his career and then to his friends (and not to his love affairs), Stanislas has a phobia of parenthood. Being a father? His worst nightmare! However, he has by his side an example of a family that works quite well. Married and already the mother of a 3 year old boy, his twin sister has just given birth to a little girl. She has not stopped working and does not intend to do so. If he recognizes that she is doing well, it is at the price of a draconian organization.

"Her children are a full-time occupation. There is no break. I can't and won't fit that into my own life."

Since a bad experience that gave him cold sweats, Stanislas is part of the "ultras", who wish to resort to radical solutions. He no longer trusts women. A girl tells him she's on the pill? Fine, but what if she's lying? Any protection is only real if he is in control, no matter how long the relationship lasts.

"If I could be sterilized, go through a vasectomy[26], I would do it. I am thinking about solutions, I am very attentive to medical discoveries in this field. A male pill is being developed, I'm looking forward to it and am willing to try it if it doesn't harm my health otherwise."

Alongside these examples of men in their thirties who are left alone by their parents and friends, or even comforted in their position, there are those who are subject to the same pressures as women in their thirties. We have already heard from Christophe, who is labelled by his parents as a "retarded

---

26. A surgical procedure that consists of ligating the vas deferens of each testicle (refer to the final glossary for a more complete definition). Contrary to many other countries in the world, particularly in Europe, vasectomy was for a long time considered as a mutilation by the French legislation. It became legal in 1999 (article 70 law n° 99-641 of 27 July 1999). Previously, article 41 of the Code of Ethics of the National Order of Physicians referred to it in these terms: "Sterilization, whether male or female, is a mutilating operation which, in the majority of cases, is not currently reversible, and whose psychological and moral consequences are unpredictable. [...] It is the physician's responsibility to assess these reasons in good conscience." Therefore, although these recommendations do not have the force of law, a surgeon who performed this operation could be sued for "assault and battery." It can now be offered for medical reasons, including in the case of an initial patient request.

teenager" and for whom his decision not to start a family remains a whim. For others, the family is more or less accusatory, allowing itself to intervene openly, or merely touching on the subject from afar. Reflections are sometimes expressed in a humorous way, "little jabs" here and there.

"Remarks are made from time to time," explains Nicolas, who has been married for four years. - Come on, it's time to think about it! - So what? When is it due? - Have you lost the instructions? - If not now, it will be too late. Etc."

Nicolas has never made having children a priority or even a goal. For the moment, his wife, whom he has known for fourteen years, does not feel ready and he does not rule out ever becoming a father.

"Some family members don't understand that we would rather travel than actually start a family. So do some friends and colleagues. My godmother had five daughters who married quickly and had children right away. She doesn't understand why, in our case, we courted for so long (fourteen years) and were still waiting after we got married."

The subject comes up regularly at family gatherings at Christmas or Easter. When I asked him if he felt judged or rejected, he said that the most scathing comment came from his professional environment:

"Judged surely, rejected I don't think. A colleague once told me that it was selfish not to have children. On the contrary, I find it very selfish to have children only to satisfy one's *ego*. I believe that there is no key age to start a family.

There are some physiological constraints, but you enjoy them differently when you have them early or late."

40 years: after that, it will be too late!

At the age of 40, opinions become clearer. The people around them and the family still want to believe that there will be a rebound; it's time for a last chance! The most optimistic ones throw out phrases in the form of a lifeline: "With the progress of medicine, you can wait a little longer. Not too long either...". Usually, the threats become more specific. "Be careful, you won't be able to afterwards, you'll regret it bitterly. You'll end up alone." Here I voluntarily conjugate the expression in the feminine. 40 years clearly mark the border between the two sexes from a physiological point of view. If before this age, women and men can boast of having and undergoing the same reasoning, from the forties onwards (sometimes even before for certain very young menopausal women), the thinking is necessarily no longer the same. The 40-year-old woman without a partner knows that she is more or less drawing a line under the possibility of conceiving, while those who, married or in a relationship, still do not want to be mothers, become aware that this decision will have irreversible consequences for the rest of their lives. This passage of midlife, even for women who have never had any doubts, is generally delicate. It is a time when all women, regardless of their background, are forced to ask themselves some questions. It is also a time for taking stock.

Isabelle, a doctor in the South of France, was frank enough to look her choice in the face at each passage of ten. She summarized the ages of her life in a very laconic way:

"I asked myself the question and said to myself that I would probably not have children. At 40, still childless, I felt no regret. At 50, it's no longer possible, and I don't regret my choice."

The only inconveniences linked to this option came from the outside. A lover of literature and philosophy, non-conformist, uninhibited, and able to talk about this subject very easily with her friends who have not followed the same path as her, she admits that she has been hurt by remarks made by men:

Among the unpleasant things, I remember some unkind comments from guys who learned that I didn't want to be a mother: "What's wrong with you? Are you afraid that pregnancy will damage your body? I could feel a small accusation of selfishness lurking behind their questions."

The suffering of some women, which sometimes turns into indifference for others, or anger, or even astonishment, comes from a quick and tenacious equation: that a woman would only be a real woman the day she becomes a mother!

Gloria, 40 years old, has never been married; she is both amused and moved by this fact:

"As a childless, unmarried woman, I am a subject of attraction for many people, including my friends. Women in my situation are seen as free electrons who are a nuisance. My current situation is a story of choice, everything seems to fit together quite well, I don't have any shortcomings, I don't feel abnormal, but it's the others who force me to look at myself differently. While I would not have naturally asked myself questions about motherhood (not having felt until then this famous maternal instinct nor the call of the biological clock), I end up questioning myself a little because of the remarks I receive from the outside. Maybe I am not normal after all? Mostly I think I'm not like everyone else, in the sense that I've made different choices than most women."

The list of prejudices faced by a woman and a man who do not want to be a mother or a father is long. They reveal a bias of the society in which we live:

"Our society is very family-oriented," says Françoise, a fifty-year-old executive assistant. "All advertisements offer and perpetuate the traditional image of the family with two children. The same goes for the magazine and women's press, which does not devote much space in its columns to childless couples; in general, it keeps out of its pages those who do not fit into the norm."

Men are also not kind to the images conveyed by the society to which they belong. Joshua points out the worm in the fruit:

"This is a taboo subject in political correctness. In order to have a great life, you absolutely have to have a stable job, be in a couple and achieve all this through children. Advertising is very standardized on this, it always represents the ideal family with a house, a child, even two - a girl, a boy -, a dog, two jobs, two cars. Motherhood is constantly praised and promoted. At the same time, it's shocking to say 'no, I'm not going to have a child' and on top of that to assume it!"

He recognizes that he is favored over his colleagues:

"There is less pressure on men. It doesn't stop with the first child, it continues afterwards. You are immediately asked, "When are you going to have your second?" There is a pernicious or outright frontal interference from those around you. I find this very unpleasant and totally inappropriate, because behind childlessness there are also sometimes problems with procreation, with infertility. When it doesn't work, it is often painful, and in this case, people don't want to shout it from the rooftops nor to spread their private life on the public place by explaining why they don't have a child. For all these reasons, I find pronatalist proselytizing unbearable!"

So much so that many do not last and end up changing course, bending under the cultural and social weight of "doing what everyone else is doing".

"I have friends who were anti-natalist and who, as they approach 40, break down and end up having a child. The famous biological clock, it seems. My older sister was on the same page as me for a long time, and then she finally had a child at 41. Now that she's a mom, she's even more interventionist than most. She tries to explain why it's great, and just because she has one and changed her mind, she wants to convert everyone around her. As far as I'm concerned, she's wasting her time, I'm not suggestible. My family tried to change my mind, especially a few years ago, now I am less porous. I am not complexed. I assume my position perfectly and I speak about it easily. My friends are tolerant, those who are intolerant are no longer friends."

Doesn't wanting children mean not loving them?

Not all people who refuse to be parents are "anti-children" either. They don't want to have any themselves, but they say they love children and like to take care of them... with all the more pleasure that they do it only from time to time.

"I have always loved children, especially babies," says Suzanne. "I used to babysit when I was a teenager and then I was an au pair. I am very protective and at the same time I don't want to let them do anything. I am very annoyed by bad children, but it is often their parents' fault!"

A woman and a man without children have multiple ways of associating with children in their environment: through their profession (like Victor, a monitor and social worker in centers for children with problems), through the family and friendship circle. It is common for someone to have a special relationship with a nephew, a niece, a godson or a goddaughter. This is the case of Vanessa with her goddaughter Emily, and Suzanne with her niece Claire. Both tell the story of how they went on vacation together several times. What are these relationships like? "I am not her mother and I refuse to be her second mother. I'm more like a friend to her," says Suzanne. For her part, Vanessa explains:

Voluntary infertility

"I am the oldest of three sisters, including twins, who each have children. My friend Nicole and I see my nieces and nephews on a regular basis, but I must admit that I am closer to some of them. I treat them almost like my daughters. When they were children, they used to come to our house during the vacations, because our house is big and we live in the country. The little ones are not really my thing. I prefer them as teenagers! When they were teenagers, my nieces were very vocal, they wanted to know everything about me and my partner, how we loved each other, what was the difference between two women. This embarrassed me a little, with respect to their parents, but also amused me!"

Sonia is godmother to her nephew. She explains how she was able to convince her brother to keep this child.

"My brother was for a long time very much in love with a woman who couldn't have children and he didn't want any. So he was very happy with this situation. She, on the other hand, suffered a lot. She was undergoing treatment for infertility. One day, she became pregnant. Obviously, for her, it was a joy without name, for our brother, it was a cataclysm! He was devastated, yet I told him to keep the baby, that he should not ask her to have an abortion, because she would resent him all her life. Today, my nephew is 15 years old and we have established a relationship of trust, a real friendly bond. Also, despite the genesis of his birth, his father is like a god to him!"

"I love kids!" exclaims Jennifer. "All my friends are having them and I don't have a problem with that. But I don't feel concerned. I know moms who don't care about other people's kids, but I do. Generally, when there are children in the room, it doesn't take me long to be surrounded by them: I have all the advantages and none of the disadvantages. I don't mind changing diapers, bottle feeding."

To love children to the point of raising and living with them when they are not your own?

"Why not?" asks Jennifer. "If there's only one! Maybe I could play mom every other weekend, but to be considered the evil stepmother of three kids who aren't hers, no thanks! A friend of mine, who would also like to have children, fell in love with a man who already has three. I told her that she was crazy and that she was heading for the wall. Chances are, this man doesn't want to be a father anymore. For a woman like me who doesn't want children, it's different. I think living with a widower would be compatible. I could consider it, just as I would consider taking care of the children of the man I love. However, if it's not a turn-off, it's a major complication and very often an obstacle in a relationship."

In general, society has always taken procreation for granted. This stance caused a Belgian author, Theophile de Giraud[27], now known as the original organizer of the Non-Parents' Day[28], to react. "You don't have a child? Be proud of it!" he writes on his blog. Hence the idea of setting up this party, half-canular, half-manifesto extremely serious translating well

---

27. GIRAUD (Théophile de), *L'Art de guillotiner les procréateurs. Manifeste anti-nataliste,* editions Le Mort-qui-trompe, 2006.
28. http://nonparents.skynetblogs.be

the fed up of a whole fringe of the population that regularly feels despised and ostracized. "Organizing a non-parents' party was intended to allow people who have made this choice to express themselves freely. It's almost a taboo subject," he says. In a world that usually praises children, let's face it, it's daring! "The conditioning on this issue is such that we often encounter hostile reactions." With his sidekick, Frédérique Longrée[29], he admits that he did it at first "to provoke[30], but then we realized that it helped those who feel monstrous for not wanting to give birth, who live it badly or who do not dare to tell their family. The party is to feel less alone."

According to Theophile de Giraud, "non-parents are the true heroes of our time" and "it is unfair that they are never celebrated as they deserve".

---

29. See her Facebook discussion group: "*I don't have children, so what?* A group for all those who, for philosophical, ethical, biological or other reasons, do not procreate and are tired of being stigmatized by this society where not having children is often associated with a defect. Our society promotes the family as a model. Many of us don't fit into that framework because we think outside the box and there are global issues that non-procreation could solve."

30. *In Libération*, dated August 6, 2010.

Chapter 3

The child obstacle

During my interviews, one word struck me because it kept coming back: "obstacle". While the profiles of the people I interviewed did not overlap at all, their vision of the child was summarized by this same word "obstacle". For them, the child would be an obstacle to turning in circles, a brake. This is a constant in their discourse. Based on this observation, I asked myself, in concrete terms, what does the child hinder?

A barrier to social and cultural development and self-actualization

"Fulfillment" has become the key word, the big thing in our rich countries. Spoiled children, my generation and even my parents' generation are or were all spoiled. My parents because they lived through the "Trente Glorieuses", a blessed time when one could choose one's job, afford the luxury of leaving one's job to find another one the next morning, and allow oneself not to plan. The seventies generally produced more cicadas than ants. Of course, there were other problems, but before the generation of AIDS and unemployment, and after the generation of our grandparents or great-grandparents who had experienced one, or even two or three, wars, the conditions of life were favorable to an evolution of customs. Thanks to this stability and to a relative economic ease, the field was free to fill other less vital needs. From then on, it was necessary to travel, to cultivate oneself, to discover who one was and to find one's way. Everyone, from the worker to the company director, is entitled to this cultural and personal development. Free museums, the development of low-cost airlines, the opening of cultural centers in the outskirts of cities are part of this phenomenon.

Raised by parents from the "Trente Glorieuses" generation, born after this blessed period, at the time of the second oil crisis (1978-1979), I hardly heard about unemployment until the nineties, when the crisis directly affected our family, when the company where my father worked suddenly went bankrupt. However, the environment in which I was raised accustomed me to the idea that a successful life requires a broad culture. You have to know the world, go to meet the Other, to exhibitions, to go to the theater, to the opera. I have developed a taste for this intellectual and geographical nomadism.

During my interviews, both men and women shared with me the same desire to travel and their fears (when not certainties) that with a child, all these beautiful projects would no longer be possible.

For them, being a parent is an obstacle to their social and cultural development and to their self-realization. They refuse to be locked up, of which the child is necessarily synonymous. They want to remain permanently connected to others and to the rest of the world.

Antoine, "an eternal child of 45 years old", has always rejected all forms of attachment, the main ones being marriage and fatherhood. If he gave in on the first point, by marrying a woman fifteen years younger than him, almost two years ago, he has not changed his mind about children and does not conceive of having any. Tall and slim, his youthful appearance is underlined by original clothing. A clown at heart, he is a player, ready to do a lot to embellish his daily life, to invent shooting stars, to create them in the eyes of his companion and his friends, to make those around him laugh and smile. Boredom! This is the real enemy of his life, against which he takes out his knight of the Round Table sword, to slay it as soon as it shows its face. The children in all this? Impossible, unthinkable! There would be one too many.

"I have seen many couples fall apart because of children. This was the case for my parents. A child is a greater or lesser dose of worry. A child cannibalizes its parents, it's so fickle: they can be adorable, and a second later, turn into a terror, throwing a big tantrum, while you are in a public

The child obstacle

place. The couple forgets that they are a couple and only sees themselves through the parental prism. Very few people can handle the shock."

The speech is not that of a clown, but of a concerned person, aware of the implications of a family.

"When I was very young, my father left and my mother took me for her husband; I had the double function of son and head of the family, which was not very healthy. Because of this, or because of it, I know the family responsibilities well. My mother was hyper-possessive, I wanted to escape her."

However, in his armor, a crack exists: Irina, his wife, a Bulgarian fairy, blonde, eccentric. His *alter ego*. At the age of 40, he began to consider a union as plausible:

"I didn't want to lose her, I found that she was really worth it to me, to face my fears. I started to reflect on myself. With her, I finally found a woman who was as playful as I was, capable of entering my world, which is rare. Rare enough for me not to let her go."

Proof that the question is not simple, even for those who are certain.

Antoine asked me never to call him at night for fear that his wife would overhear our conversation. He knows that this subject is likely to become more and more sensitive in the future. It has become taboo. Irina is now 30 years old and although she has never before expressed a desire to have children, he feels that she is changing.

"When we pass friends with children, she looks at them with different eyes, she sometimes lingers on the street at little ones or when we pass by children's store windows. This could become problematic for my marriage, but it's always a failure to get people to change. Marriage is a time bomb: at some point, one is bound to disappoint the other. My wife knew where she stood, I never hid the truth about my conception of family from her."

Ten years ago, Antoine, who had moved to Great Britain, was in a relationship with an English woman he adored. When the question of children arose, he found a very radical solution.

"We loved each other sincerely, I also liked her parents very much, I felt good with her. All this collapsed the day she clearly presented me with a choice: we could get married, have children, or separate. Becoming a mother, even more than getting married, was an obsession for her, an ultimate goal, an accomplishment, she believed. I think she was like many English women, culturally formatted, for whom not having children at 25 is experienced as a catastrophe. So we parted by mutual agreement, knowing that our views were irreconcilable. She got married shortly afterwards to an Englishman who seemed to me to be a caricature: he likes beer, soccer, goes to matches with his mates, even goes on vacation without her. I think she's happy because she has what she wanted most, but I don't think her relationship fulfills her or fulfills her as it could."

For Antoine, this refusal to be a father clearly goes hand in hand with a lifestyle based on freedom.

"I get a kick out of people judging others on their appearance. We are in a world where everyone puts a label on you. I wanted to get away from any pressure, whether it was family, social or financial. I left home when I was 20, first to Britain and then to the United States. I have always spoken English well and have known England since I was 14. I have a younger brother who is four years younger than me. He, too, felt the need to move abroad: today he lives in Berlin."

Mary's speech, although a little different in form, is quite close to Antoine's. Both assume a small part of selfishness:

"For the moment, I have plans for travel and decoration. I want to play it cool, I've given up my Judeo-Christian complex. On the other hand, I'm not just focused on myself either, I give literacy classes against illiteracy, one weekend every three weeks."

Stanislas does not plan to have children one day either, entirely focused on his professional ambition and his bachelor pleasures:

"Along with work, the most important value in life for me is friendship, not love. I am very faithful in friendship, not in love. I prefer to go on vacation with friends than with my girlfriend. It's less restrictive, I have more fun. I prefer them to everything else. My current girlfriend (previous ones too) blames me, I spend more time with them than with her."

Moreover, since he was traumatized at age 19 by his experience with his then-girlfriend, he no longer trusts women:

"She told me one day, out of the blue, that she had a late period and that if it turned out she was pregnant, she would keep the child. For me, nothing could be worse than this news. I was so desperate that I began to think of the worst possible outcomes, I told myself that I would just kill myself, if it turned out that my girlfriend was pregnant."

The test results arrived: negative! Relief is followed by anger. Stanislas immediately breaks up with his girlfriend and swears that no girl will ever do this to him again.

"I've become adamant about this: I warn the girls I'm dating. If one of them had a child behind my back, I would refuse to acknowledge it, to take care of it or even to see it! That would make me run away. It's not a way to keep me."

This lack of trust prevents him from having long relationships (which he seems not to want either). How to live on an equal footing in fear of the other? Stanislas now sees all women as liars, traitors, egg-layers, "ready for anything". He thus prepares the ground for successive failures in love, opens the door to many misunderstandings. Behind all this, isn't there also a fear of falling in love? Has he ever fallen for a woman to the point of hesitating or changing his mind?

"No. I had a long relationship of two years, it ended because of this issue. When the girl realized that I would not change my mind."

Miles away, despite having a very different personality and life from Stanislas, Joshua thinks and behaves in much the same way:

"I have not had any sentimental encounters so far that could have changed my mind. I go to older women, for whom the question of a child no longer arises. That frees me up."

To feel unique, to be pampered, to never have to answer to anyone, to refuse an invitation to stay at home and watch a

The child obstacle

DVD, to leave on a whim to see the sea, for a weekend of skiing or a hike in the mountains with no other concern than packing a suitcase. I agree with Stanislas when he says: "I like the idea of not having any time constraints, of being able to go away for the weekend whenever I want. I have friends who live at the same pace as me and we regularly meet up in the four corners of Europe." Stanislas is certainly not the only one to put friendship on a pedestal. It is one of the characteristics of the lifestyle of thirty and forty year olds who are "single" (just look at the television series that reflect this state of mind, *Friends* in particular).

I can't help but project myself. When I have a baby, will we still have our mornings? My friends who are already mothers have warned me: the clock radio will become useless, the cries of the child will be enough. No more sleeping in, I feel as if Marie, one of the most anti-children young women I've ever interviewed, is whispering in my ear: "I warned you! Say goodbye to your peace of mind!" This prospect makes me shudder: how do you manage to stand up every morning at 6 a.m.? At the same time, thousands of women and couples do this, so why shouldn't I? Is the argument strong enough to justify not having a child?

A professional obstacle

On the question of work-maternity, surveys conducted by INED, among others, tell us that in France, three quarters of women between the ages of 20 and 49 work[31]. This average varies greatly according to the life cycle, particularly when the first child arrives. The *Families and Employers* survey[32] has made it possible to monitor the professional activity of parents when a birth occurs. The consequences are manifold: they range from a total interruption of work to a simple shift in working hours, including the taking of part-time work. "Among women born between 1955 and 1985 who have had at least one child, nearly 4 out of 10 were not working before a birth and 5 out of 10 the year after. The number of unemployed women, whether they are inactive, on parental leave or unemployed, increases with each birth. Thirty percent of them were not working before the first birth, 37 percent before the second birth and 54 percent before the third. The following year, 38% were not working after the first birth, 51% after the second and 69% after the third[33]." However, the arrival of a child does not automatically mean that a woman has to give up her job for good: after two years, more than one woman in two resumes her job.

As far as fathers are concerned, the changes are minor. In the twelve months following a birth, their professional situation remains virtually the same: only 6% of them, again according to the INED survey, report that their activity has undergone

---

31. National Institute of Demographic Studies.

32. Conducted by INED in 2004-2005 in metropolitan France among 9,745 men and women aged 20 to 49 and their employers. See in particular the site *"Family and employers" survey 2005*, https://efe.web.ined.fr/

33. PAILHÉ (Ariane) and SOLAZ (Anne), "Vie professionnelle et naissance : la charge de la conciliation repose essentiellement sur les femmes", *op. cit.*

The child obstacle

changes (status, hours, reorganization, or withdrawal from the labor market). The only point that really varies for men concerns changes in working hours without a change in working time: 30% of fathers are affected, compared to 7% of mothers. In fact, for mothers, the adjustment of schedules is more to the detriment of the length of working time (22% of them). "The types of adjustment also differ according to the level of education. The less educated are more likely to leave the labor market than the others, who tend to reduce their activity or their working hours." Financial status also plays a role: more single mothers or mothers with an unemployed spouse return to work than mothers with a partner who earns well. If we go into a little more detail, the arrival of a child is an even more restrictive and negative factor professionally when they were on a fixed-term contract or professionally unstable. "Women on fixed-term contracts are more likely to stop working than those on permanent contracts. Those without a work contract (self-employed or family helpers) are less likely to reduce their professional commitment. We find that mothers working in the public sector reduce their working hours while those in the private sector often quit their jobs."

This last information is in line with what I frequently heard from my interviewees. Women who are most often employed in the private sector, they have a desire to pursue their careers according to their ambition or their nomadism. In the first case, the arrival of a child would disrupt their professional ascent, in the second case it would force them to stabilize, which does not suit their character. I am thinking in particular of Gloria, a very beautiful brunette in her forties, originally from Latin America. She arrived in France at the age of 19 to pursue her studies and decided to make a life for herself. Her slightly tanned skin and her chocolate-colored mid-length hair are undoubtedly an asset, but she never plays with it and as we talk, I notice that she tries to erase this involuntary seduction by rigor and self-control. With her, it is obvious, *business is business*. She works in a large press and public relations agency, as head of the *corporate* division (management consulting, fair trade). After having worked in advertising and invented many slogans herself, she now supervises a team in charge of working on the human side. She now responds to clients by identifying their personality. She adapts easily to a new environment, as she likes change and challenge. If a feeling of repetition creeps in, boredom is the first sign that she wants to leave or change direction.

"I'm a chronic dissatisfier, changing companies every three years. This mobility has certainly prevented me from digging my hole somewhere and moving up the corporate ladder. By constantly moving to new horizons, I miss out on political maneuvering, miss out on opportunities such as positions that are only available after several years of loyal service. I could also have become a partner in a company, but I don't want to. I prefer to keep my freedom. To be able to leave whenever I want, wherever I want. If tomorrow I want to go back to Argentina, it's possible; if I have an opportunity in Rome, Italy, I pack my bags and fly. No regrets."

The child obstacle

Freedom and independence, these are her main desires, her life line. Gloria is not only a *no kid*, she is also single. By personal choice. She is a very self-controlled woman, square, logical and intelligent. She has priorities, has known how to prioritize them and, even better, how to express them, and then to align her life with them. Motherhood was not one of them.

One of the conclusions of this vast INED survey once again proves childless women right: "Mother or not, stop as little as possible," a human resources manager told me, "especially if you want to climb the ladder and stay in the race for high-potential positions." Generally speaking, the women who are best integrated into the labor market are those who decrease their professional activity the least. It is true that the law protects women employees when they are pregnant, but afterwards there is no guarantee that they will be able to return to an equally interesting position or that their superiors will not make them "pay" for their absence.

Roxanne decided to take advantage of the birth of her second child to take a one-year parental leave. She extended it again for a year and in the meantime had a third child. Now, after almost four years out of the workforce, she wants to return to work and has asked her company, where she is officially still employed, to reinstate her. Her company has no legal right to refuse her, but there are no vacancies and the human resources department is turning the issue on its head to "fit her in". "I'm afraid they'll end up offering me a severance package," Roxanne sighs. "A solution that scares me more than anything else, because then, how can I present myself on the job market and go apply to other companies that don't know me, and justify the fact that I've devoted four years to my family, including raising my children?"

A friend of mine said, "Any mother of twins who applies for a job should automatically be hired, because managing two babies at the same time is such an extraordinary feat." When you have children, you have a double agenda. "Double trouble", Marie cynically says to me. When will I be able to read and write, if I have to pick up a baby, who is a permanent guest in my home, from the nursery at 6 p.m., then give him a bath, feed him, play with him, read him one or more stories to put him to sleep? Will I have to give up my dreams of being a journalist-writer-manager-entrepreneur-librarian-publisher to be a perfect mother?

The "childless", especially women, answer this question in the negative. Being able to change jobs at will, moving on a whim or as soon as a tempting professional offer is made to you: this refusal of sedentariness is a more assertive argument for them, because when a couple with children moves[34], it is almost always the woman who gives up her job to follow her husband. Motherhood is thus considered by a very large number of women (even among those who have become mothers) to be a hindrance to professional success,

---

34. Pailhé (Ariane) and Solaz (Anne), "Vie professionnelle et naissance : la charge de la conciliation repose essentiellement sur les femmes", *op. cit.*

The child obstacle

and this is a fundamental key to understanding the perception of gender inequality.

Another argument that keeps coming up in the mouths of the "childless" is the sharing of tasks within the couple. In order to understand what is holding women back from having children, we need to look at the French reality with regard to household chores. The survey conducted by Arnaud Régnier-Loilier shows that the birth of a child accentuates a situation that is already highly alienating for women. As a general rule, "women (mothers or not) assume 80% of domestic tasks in France and the imbalance is all the more pronounced the more children there are in the family and the younger the child. In 2005[35], among women in couples aged 20 to 49, 8 out of 10 "always" or "most often" do the ironing, 7 out of 10 do the meal preparation, half do the vacuuming and grocery shopping and 4 out of 10 do the dishes and bookkeeping."

Why does the arrival of a child reinforce these inequalities? First of all, as Arnaud Régnier-Loilier points out, because "professional adjustments mainly affect women". As we have seen above, quite a few women reduce or stop working (in 25% of cases if it is a first child, 32% of cases if it is an additional child). The less a woman works, the more she will take on the daily household tasks. Once again, it is clear that if a woman does not want to take on the domestic aspect of the home, it is better for her not to work at home or reduce her working hours.

---

35. Erfi survey, *Study of family and intergenerational relations*, conducted by Arnaud Régnier-Loilier of INED.

Marie, to whom I have already given the floor several times previously, is particularly flayed on this subject. For her, this aspect of motherhood is essential, certainly given her family upbringing. She knows that being a mother means taking care of her home more than a childless woman would normally do.

"My only constraints are guided by the arrival of my husband's children once a month. We have them every third weekend and half of the vacations. I am in no way a substitute mother: I don't care about them - they are nice, but at 7 and 5 years old, exchanges are limited when they are not without interest. On the other hand, I play my role as a vestal virgin when they are here, which is to manage the daily routine, meals, etc., so that Martin can spend as much time as possible with them. Nobody asks me to do this, but it seems normal to me. It's a family atavism, no doubt about it."

The second important point highlighted by this survey is the reaction of women to this imbalance. It turns out (not very surprisingly!) that a majority of them are not satisfied with this division of labor. Even more worrying is that their level of satisfaction *decreases* as they have more children: "While 30% of women without children gave a score of less than 8 out of 10, this proportion rises to 40% for mothers with two children and almost 50% for those with three or more children. The number of children, on the other hand, had no effect on men's satisfaction." Should we conclude that mothers with children are less happy than women without children?

The child obstacle

Sometimes motherhood is also almost completely incompatible with the activity carried out by women. The champion cyclist Jeannie Longo confided on this point in a book, *Jeannie by Longo*[36]. "When I look back on my career, I can't regret anything. I would have liked to have had children, but it was my body that did not follow. I believe that the body makes its own physical choices. I compensate for this lack by mothering my loved ones a lot[37]!" Many professions make it difficult to "want" and above all to "be able" to have a child: the great reporters, brought to cover conflicts all around the world, often have difficulty not only to raise children, but simply to conceive them. War and its atrocities - even if journalists are not the direct victims, but the witnesses - weaken women physiologically. Florence Shaal and Marine Jacquemin have each worked for TF1 for nearly thirty years, covering news in Darfur, Somalia, Afghanistan, Iraq, Chechnya, Cambodia, etc., all regions of the world where there are harsh conflicts. Traveling all the time is not conducive to marriage or having a child. Florence Shaal ended up adopting a little girl in Vietnam[38], while Marine Jacquemin created in 2001 the association Enfants afghans with the support of La Chaîne de l'Espoir, Muriel Robin and Claire Chazal in order to finance and build a hospital, the French Medical Institute for Children in Kabul. While being "maternal", neither of them chose

---

36. LONGO (Jeannie), *Jeannie by Longo*, Le Cherche-Midi éditions, Paris, 2010.
37. Interview given to the magazine *Femme actuelle* (n° 1336, May 2010).
38. SHAAL (Florence), *Recherche enfant passionnément*, J.-C. Lattès, Paris, 1997.

to give up their career as a great reporter to start a family. They wanted to continue to practice a profession they believed in and loved while getting as close as possible to an unfulfilled desire.

After all these feminine words, it is time to listen again to a man on this subject. If it is true that women are the first to be affected professionally, men are not or no longer left out and are aware, for the most part, of the change in the rhythm of life that a birth induces. For Stanislas, this is inconceivable.

"My twin sister is a mom: she has a 3 year old boy and a newborn girl; she manages to do it with a lot of organization. She's not trying to convince me, she's happy the way she is and I have to admit that she's doing pretty well. She manages to manage her children, while working. However, as far as I am concerned, I really enjoy my job and I work a lot, between twelve and seventeen hours a day. At peak times, I start around 6 a.m. and sometimes finish at midnight. This pace makes it difficult for me to think about anything else, to do sports, to go out, to go away for the weekend. I manage to see my friends, but I give them top priority over everything else as soon as I have a window of opportunity outside my office. Without even talking about a child, I already have trouble projecting myself into a lasting relationship, so being a father is simply unthinkable!"

The child obstacle

An obstacle to nomadic love

In this paragraph, I would like to focus on women and men who are not involved in any form of lasting relationship. *At first glance,* surveys and civil status records place them in the category of "singles". This word is a Pandora's box! Between the uptight, shy, bitterly inclined single person and the "bachelor", the definition that seems most appropriate here is that of an individual who feels comfortable with his or her single status, who has chosen it and not been forced into it, who takes advantage of it to have adventures, who earns a good enough living that finances are not a problem, and who navigates society with pride and a blatant ease. Single people are more numerous in the cities, especially the big cities, than in the countryside. Why is this? Simply because the urban environment, the fabric offered by a big city, allows them to blend in, to be invisible to those who might spy on them (family in particular, their professional hierarchy, their childhood friends).

Nothing predicts that the single woman will remain "alone" or "single" all her life, but she ignores all the prejudices that have long been attached to the old girl. The concept of Catherinette, a tradition perpetuated by hatters, is no longer flattering. Today, unmarried girls at 25 are legion and it is no longer an oddity or a tare. In 2007, the age of first marriage was 31.5 for men and 29.5 for women. At 25, there is no danger in the house, even for those who want to get married and start a family at all costs!

Personally, I lived this period in an ambivalent way: what happiness to be free when you are courted, when you feel master of your life, of your love choices and when you are not subjected to any external pressure! Some milestones, some anniversaries, are, let's admit it, more difficult to pass, when suddenly around you are many couples. Apart from these blues and slumps, the advantages are numerous. Going on vacation with friends and coming back with the memory of a beautiful love affair, locking yourself away for several weeks to live a passion that you know is fleeting, but which galvanizes you for several months...

Without children, it is easy to fly from one story to another, to constantly change your mind and follow your instincts from day to day! Today, being single is no longer synonymous with loneliness. Love life is one of the essential components of these female and male trajectories. Donjuanism is the other word to describe this intense love and/or sexual activity.

"I like to flirt, to meet people, to meet new people, to be available. I don't hide it too much. The life of a seducer, a distinguished dilettante, suits me. No attachment, no passionate drama! I prefer a certain quality of life," Stanislas emphatically declares.

Women and men choose to be nomadic in love, just as others choose to be nomadic in their work. Sometimes, the two are in agreement. In these cases, autonomy is strongly claimed. It is an object of pride. For them, life with two people is not only unattractive, but is perceived as incompatible with their self-image. I often hear people say to me in the form of

The child obstacle

a conclusion: "I am not made for life as a couple. My personal space suffers too much. I need some fresh air and a change."

Roland Jaccard, disciple of Cioran, Schopenhauer and *Bartleby*, offers an extreme vision of the human being. For him, it is a crime to give birth: "Giving life makes us criminals, because life is a gigantic mistake."

Of all the people I interviewed, I think I can say that he was the one who most shocked me. Although he was jovial and extremely sympathetic, he told me the worst truths with an incredible lightness. His vision of life is black, cynical: he readily admits to being a nihilist. But he is not a misanthrope. His favorite sin? Women! Young women precisely and especially not one, not two, not three... but all of them!

"There are a number of things that are prohibitive for me: for example, I don't like women my age. I'm more attracted to young women, even very young women for whom the question of having children has not yet arisen. Secondly, I am not attracted to women who are fat or who put on weight for X or Y reasons. I don't like the idea that a woman's body is changing."

When I ask him how to fight the natural aging of the skin, organs and mind, and if he advocates surgical interventions, he replies with a smile:

"It's something you want to avoid all the time and at all costs. When I was younger, I was never attracted to middle-aged women. I was not a gerontophile and I still am not."

More precisely, children, even when envisaged with a younger woman, are always out of the question. Roland

Jaccard addresses here a dimension that has not yet been raised: that of fidelity in the couple, if not of body, at least of heart and mind, a foundation often considered unavoidable in the consecrated model of the family.

"To have children is to found a family, which includes a series of constraints; it is also to start from the idea that one will stay with the woman with whom one has committed this crime, the one who is or will be the mother of one's children. It is thus to question the question of fidelity. But nothing exists over time. Life is ephemeral."

Fidelity is one of the pillars of marriage, inscribed as such in the declaration of intention that the priest asks the future couple to write, recalled at the moment of the exchange of consent. However, there is no Code of Parenthood... no contract at the moment of the birth of a child that the parents would sign committing themselves to each other for eternity. If there is a contract, it is rather a moral one. The Family Code requires that parents take care of their children with dignity until they reach the age of majority, providing them with material assistance, food, adequate care, and access to school. What about love? Is it not desirable to be a couple registered in the duration when one wants to be parents? As Roland Jaccard suggests, there is a causal link between the two. In his logic, if he does not believe in fidelity or in the permanence of feelings and in the durability of a couple, it seems more honest to him not to procreate.

A thesis that others will not necessarily follow...

The child obstacle

An obstacle to true love

"When a woman enters motherhood, the risk is to see her only as a mother and not as a lover," Joshua tells me, which perfectly sums up the feeling shared by many of my participants.

Thus, motherhood damages love relationships, even if all the "childless" are, of course, not followers of Donjuanism, swearing only by the ephemeral. Some, on the contrary, are in love for the long term. Children, instead of becoming the outcome of this love, are then perceived as "love killers": "If a child arrives, we will love each other less intensely, we will have to share with him or her." Not only does the arrival of a child introduce a third person into the pairing, risking to seriously unbalance it, and in the long run perhaps to make it explode, but this new little person needs to be protected and loved more than the "big people" who surround him or her. There is no excuse for not taking care of a baby. This fragile being par excellence is an attention grabber and an absolutely exhausting energy catalyst. In these conditions, the risk is to pay less and less attention to your partner. Of course, this trap is also present in couples without children, but it is stronger for parents. Many divorces have their source in this progressive disintegration.

For some people, it is totally impossible for a child to break the desire for exclusivity, which is the ultimate proof of true crazy love. Sometimes there is also the fear of not loving the child who will interfere in the couple, of making him pay for being there.

To illustrate this fusion of love, the refusal to share the object of his passion, I would like to tell the story of Claude Schlienger. This psychotherapist of about sixty years wished that I did not disguise her identity. Assuming her history, one feels that she is ready to fight with anyone who would oppose her.

This was certainly the most difficult, but also the most rewarding interview I have ever done. Armed with her long experience as a psychotherapist, Claude has a significantly different view of the subject than the other women I had the opportunity to discuss with. The question of motherhood challenges her and interests her. She did not need me to think about it at length. Everything suggests to me that her actions in general are the result of reflection. Unusually for me, she wanted our conversation to take place in her apartment. However, when I arrive, I am surprised by her icy attitude. It is obvious to me that she will not give herself up without me giving her something from me first. She wants something to grind, explanations about my project and the way I will do it. She is on the defensive: is the subject still too sensitive for her to talk about it calmly? Is it more sensitive than she thought? Claude is used to listening and today, it is she who must confide in me. The roles are reversed and I can feel how this complicates things.

We begin to talk in short bursts. I fumble, she relaxes. Her position on the question of children is not categorical, but on the contrary, full of nuances. One point, however, remains intangible and makes her angry: the idea that "a woman

The child obstacle

in society would only exist through her status as a married woman, through her children and grandchildren."

"In any society, when one meets a woman who is no longer a young girl, she is invariably asked the same questions to get acquainted: "Are you married and do you have children?" On trips, at dinner parties, this is a recurring question. Today, I'm more likely to be asked if I have grandchildren, as I would be old enough to be a grandmother. I have never felt I had to justify my choices and I never have. I am just amazed at the stupidity of people who put you in boxes. Only once did I lie about it. I got so fed up with the question that kept coming up, I said one day that my children were all on public assistance. The person couldn't think of anything to say to me because she was so stuck in her place."

Since she is addressing this aspect of non-motherhood, I take the opportunity to ask her opinion in a broader sense. If she doesn't feel criticized or at fault for not wanting a child, for even having an abortion, why do some childless women feel guilt?

"Because society sends them this image. We are only a woman if we have a child. I agree that it is natural to have a child because our body is ready for it, we have a device to conceive it, but when you consider that a child is the most precious thing in the world, this justification is not enough. I wasn't going to make a child just because I could. I know a woman who had five children because she loved being pregnant. That's five children damaged for life! Yes, we are programmed to have periods, and to bring babies into the world. But having children for whom, for what, how? These are the real questions. What is wonderful is the idea of transmission. You have to be able to give. I can't stand the *people* in the newspapers who have their photos taken with their offspring, just to be like everyone else. On the contrary, it's true that women without children can be puzzling, incomprehensible, disturbing, and also frightening, because they don't belong to a traditional pattern, they are outside the box. They are above all very free. However, it is not for this reason that I did not have children. It is a consequence. I didn't have a child because I didn't think it was possible."

Now that trust is established between us, I try to dig a little deeper into her childhood. Did she see herself as a mother when she was younger? When did she begin to see a change in herself?

"As a teenager, I wanted many children. However, I had parents who were so passionately in love that for me, having a child with a man I liked, but who would not have been the whole universe for me, seemed impossible. My parents were very much in love, but my mother was more of a wife than a mother: in this, I had the most wonderful mother in the world. She gave me a taste for love and freedom and not for that exclusive and fusional bond that sometimes revolts me between mothers and their children. Sometimes you see mothers and grandparents who would literally eat their children if they could, and often they eat them completely, figuratively this time. Our mother loved us, but gave us our place as children. This image has remained strongly anchored

The child obstacle

in me. My father died when I was 9 years old. My mother held on for us, but she died when she saw that I was independent. She brought me to adulthood, I graduated and she left a few months later. My brother didn't have a child either, his wife didn't want one."

The vision of her parents "passionately in love with each other" forged in her a foundation of a solidity that proved to be without fault. We see in her that the couple is synonymous with crazy love, longevity, fidelity to the memory, all things that she has taken over and perpetuated in her own life. Today, the man of her life, with whom she lived for thirty-nine years, has died. There is not a day that goes by that she does not think of him, that she does not honor what he was. However, this man was never, in the eyes of the law, her "husband": already married to another woman and father of three children, he always refused to divorce and abandon his legitimate wife. Preferring to make his affair with Claude public and official, he made sure that his two wives knew of each other's existence. A company director, very much in love with Claude, he lived a very long physical and intellectual passion with her, without feeling that he was abandoning his family.

"We lived together for thirty-nine years. In the end, I was with my partner much more often than most of my friends, because when we were together, we were together completely, fully, for four days. Many married women don't see their husbands on a daily basis, as he travels, comes home in the night from work. I reproduced what my mother had left me: the crazy love with a man. I preferred my way of life to all the mediocre lives I saw around me, or to those I had lived before. For me, love is above everything else: money, social success."

Certainly, her couple does not resemble most of the models that one meets in a life. Claude could have chosen to have a child with this man she adored.

"I was pregnant with his child twice, but because he was married and didn't want to divorce his children, we didn't want to have any together. The first time I got pregnant, I didn't tell him, because we had just met. Also, I was a nurse at the time, and I was too afraid that he would think it was intentional, that I might have intentionally gotten pregnant in order to force him to divorce. This was not the case. At that time, having an abortion was terrible, because it was still illegal. Most French women went to England for abortions. It was horrible, I didn't speak English. You are lucky, women of your generation, not to have experienced that. I became pregnant a second time, five years later. But I was on the pill. This time, I talked to him about it and we hesitated a lot. He let me choose, saying this wonderful phrase: 'Do as you wish.' On my side, I had already decided, made my appointment with the gynecologist. I did not keep the child voluntarily."

I am puzzled: why would a woman decide not to keep a child of the man she loves? And how could leaving her the choice seem wonderful to Claude? Didn't making this decision alone seem to her to be a crushing weight?

The child obstacle

"I loved him too much. In a normal couple, having a child would have seemed like a great gift, but in my situation it wasn't. If my child had been sick, and this was the time when I had to see his father, I would have had to go without to take care of him. Impossible, I think I would have thrown him out the window! I loved this man too much to sacrifice the time I had with him to a child. Then, in relation to his children, the situation would have been difficult, complicated. He already had three, and it would have meant giving him an extra burden, an extra worry. I thought it would have been very selfish of me, even if the problem was not financial. This child would have been deprived of his father insofar as my companion did not really live with me, he would not have lived with him either. I, who had suffered so much from not having a father, did not want to put my child through that. Afterwards, we often talked about the child that we had not had together, but that we could have had: our son. It could only have been a son, of course," she laughed, with sobs in her voice. What would this little man or woman from the two of us have looked like?

Later, much later, she would tell me in conversation that a third time she thought she was pregnant again. A small sentence between two others.

"That time," she adds, "I probably would have had a harder time not keeping him, refusing that child again. This time, it would have been a harder decision to make."

And then, fate, or something else, decided otherwise making things suddenly simpler: there was no child, false alarm.

"On the other hand, if I hadn't met F., having a child alone would never have been an option either. In my eyes, a child could only be envisaged with the right partner, that would have been the icing on the cake. I don't regret anything. I can't regret something that doesn't exist. I don't know what it would have been like. So it's not a sensitive subject: as long as you have made a choice, it's assumed. The only regret is the curiosity we had about this child: what would have become of him. We joked about it. F. regretted it. It was more a curiosity than a real lack. In general, I think that the child is not respected enough; parents project their own desires, wishes and fears onto them. On the contrary, the child is a little free man."

Chapter 4

Mater dolorosa: being pregnant, a hell?

"If we told the butchery, sorry happiness, that it is, well, humanity could be extinguished in just fifty years."

Florence FORESTI in her sketch
Pregnancy.

The refusal of physical transformations and other inconveniences

Not to get fat, not to become another woman... this fear of seeing one's body change leads to the question of self-confidence, of the love relationship and of seduction. This fear is also present in men who do not like to see their wife and lover change, even for a given period of time, abhor the bodies that expand, and bear very badly the hormonal changes acting on the mood: "a pregnant woman is boring!"

Before becoming a parent and experiencing the thousand and one responsibilities (and annoyances) that come with this new status, before going through and undergoing the throes of childbirth, a (long) nine-month period is on the horizon for all mothers-to-be and of course, let's not forget about them, the fathers-to-be. Pregnancy is described by some as a wonderful time, and by others as hell.

Among the "childless", it is extremely common to come across those who consider pregnancy to be an abyss, a succession of bad news, blows of fate, trials worthy of the Stone Age.

"I love Florence Foresti's sketch on pregnant women," says Marie, one of my most adamant speakers. "She exposes reality so well! In my opinion, she does not use caricature at all. For example, when she talks about the secrecy of childbirth - 'You didn't know? We are not allowed to tell you, we young mothers, we are bound by maternal secrecy. They make us sign a confidentiality clause when we leave the maternity ward' - because otherwise no woman would want to have children anymore!"

Let's be clearer, if I had to summarize what I heard on the subject, the recriminations revolve around: the vagabond and execrable mood of the future mothers, the breasts that look like road maps, the legs like electric poles, the recurrent nausea, the brain that suddenly softens to the point of transforming a Nobel Prize of mathematics into a Barbie suffering from Alzheimer's disease, without forgetting the multiple kilos that propel the prettiest size 38 into size 42 or 44. Who has never heard a pregnant woman say, "Watch out, get out of the way, here comes the whale" (when they're not being called a sperm whale!)? For Marie, being pregnant is a "violation of the integrity of the body".

"It disgusts me. A fetus is an alien in the womb that deforms our feet, legs and arms. Even the primogeniture is often the source of a catastrophic weight gain. I don't want to play this lottery, I don't want to look like a whale. I remember my sister, who is really a beautiful girl - she is 5'8" and has always been slim - but she has a bad venous return. The result? It was horrible, she swelled up like a balloon and suffered throughout her pregnancy. Personally, I get fat just by looking at a pickle. When I was little, I was more than curvy and struggled to have a standard figure. I value my looks and I attach great importance to them. Moreover, it is out of the question for me to impose my hormonal and physical transformations on my boyfriend: to be in a bad mood all the time, or to have a depressive tendency, like many pregnant women. No way! I leave that to others!"

Another argument to put in the rank of the sacrifices linked to pregnancy: having to adopt a strict diet.

"The ambient hygienism and catastrophism forbidding you to drink raw milk camembert and no alcohol, I can't imagine going without rosé champagne for nine months! Yes, I assume my choice loud and clear."

Mater dolorosa: being pregnant, a hell?

For all women, remove from the menu all alcoholic beverages, as well as raw milk cheeses (risk of catching listeriosis), raw meat and fish (goodbye sushi and smoked salmon, beef carpaccio and tartar) and cold cuts (rillettes, pâtés and jellied products). The icing on the cake for those who are not immune to toxoplasmosis - that is to say, about 50% of French women today - is that meat must be ultra-cooked and raw vegetables washed with white vinegar; when doctors do not simply order salads in restaurants or do not touch any lamb's lettuce leaf that has not been washed five times beforehand by yourself. A golden rule: a woman should not trust anyone. Not even her mother or her best friend. In addition, a blood test must be done once a month to make sure that the patient has not contracted toxoplasmosis without her knowledge, since the symptoms are often so subtle that it is difficult to detect them.

Apart from these prohibitions, let's not forget that the pregnant woman - definitely a species apart - has the wonderful surprise of becoming prone to nausea and vomiting, especially frequent in the first trimester, to food "cravings" that are as furious as they are sudden and to severe and uncontrollable disgust.

"When my sister was pregnant, you couldn't ask her to cook a single meal," recalls Marc. "I remember the last vacation we all spent together, it got a little tiring for everyone. My mother would try to find dishes that suited her, but if she was unlucky enough to make a mistake and fall short, or if cooking smells bothered her when she got there, it was quite a drama!"

Finally, there are few women who do not experience heartburn and acid reflux from the seventh month of pregnancy. These inconveniences, which are more or less well tolerated depending on the woman, easily explain the deterioration of her mood (we agree that it is not very pleasant to be permanently bloated, constipated or to feel one's stomach suffering from daily reflux).

The fear of suffering during childbirth

"Childbirth is barbaric and cruel!" Is it possible to measure the level of pain felt at that moment when you have never given birth? We all think about it or have thought about it at least once, and the prospect makes many women shudder. So much so, that some of us would never go through with it. Even the super-moms who swear by natural childbirth and the extraordinary power of sophrology dread this moment.

Birth is surrounded by a halo of mystery, we always hear the same things, the same stories, but finally, modesty or a certain desire to keep all this under the seal of secrecy, prevents us from telling in detail what *exactly* a woman has just experienced. There are those who know, who have lived it, and those who do not know. Between the two, a fracture line is drawn: impassable. A third category "knows" what to expect without necessarily having experienced it: the medical profession (obstetricians, nurses, midwives, surgeons). If you are not a doctor, you have no idea of the extent of the carnage,

Mater dolorosa: being pregnant, a hell?

the deliverance and the happiness. The words attached to this experience are raw, harsh, or on the contrary, excessively positive. They convey all the unreasonable fears and fantasies that a birth brings.

Generally, those who know don't talk. "The women who are easy to talk to in public are the ones who have suffered the least," said a friend of mine who had already had two children. That day, I had to be satisfied with this laconic sentence. All women have experienced pain, but not at the same level.

"Rite of passage", trial by fire, the suffering that accompanies the birth of a child is an obligatory fact of life that has been mitigated for only a few decades by a local anesthetic, the famous epidural. Why, under these conditions, do women continue to be afraid? "Because there is no such thing as 100% in medicine," says a gynecologist at a hospital in the Paris region, during the childbirth preparation meetings she organizes in front of an audience of confused and insecure future parents. "In obstetrics, even more than in other specialties, 2 + 2 does not make 4", she has been hammering on for twenty years. First of all, it takes a minimum of time to administer the product. Between the moment when the woman arrives at the maternity ward and the moment when she is going to expel her child, about an hour must pass to ensure that all the conditions are met: to check that the patient is able to receive the injection of an anesthetic. Then, neither the epidural nor the cesarean section prevent contractions... Finally, once you embark on the adventure, you are not sure of anything. If you have a skin infection in the area where the injection is made, if you have an anthrax or an abscess, if your temperature exceeds 38 °C, if you have strong coagulation disorders or even certain herniated discs, the anesthesiologist will refuse to give you an epidural. The same is true if your labor is too advanced or if you are too close to delivery. "If you arrive at the hospital and your cervix is already dilated beyond 7 [a scale of 1 to 10, 10 being the maximum dilation possible, allowing the baby to pass], you can say goodbye to the epidural; it will not be administered." Admittedly, the expulsion of the newborn is then in itself quite quick (half an hour), but the contractions that accompany labor last on average between 5 and 8 hours. It is not a pleasure for any woman, even the most enduring.

Other forms of assistance to relieve the mother-to-be is possible: gaseous liquid or spinal anesthesia that numbs the lower half of the body, similar to the epidural. The effect is faster, but the mother-to-be is more likely to have a hypotensive accident. A local anesthetic can also be used. This is an injection of analgesic into the muscles of the perineum that does not eliminate the pain due to contractions, but reduces the pain of an episiotomy[39] when it is necessary. There are also non-medical methods: acupuncture or relaxation and breathing techniques such as sophrology, haptonomy and

---

39. A surgical procedure that consists of opening the perineum during childbirth by cutting with scissors in order to let the child pass through. In 2002-2003, 47.3% of women who gave birth by natural means had to undergo an episiotomy. This operation is more common among primiparous women - 68% of them - than among multiparous women - 31%.

Mater dolorosa: being pregnant, a hell?

massages. These are all preparation methods that help to better bear the pain. Many women, however, laugh and scoff at these beautiful methods.

"Sophrology? I had dutifully followed all my childbirth preparation classes, but on the day, when the contractions started to make themselves felt, I didn't think of anything else but the epidural. I wanted the anesthesiologist to give it to me immediately, I couldn't wait another minute, and I forgot everything that I thought I had wisely and religiously integrated for hours! The imaginary flame that I was supposed to visualize to help me breathe, I couldn't see it at all.

"When the anesthesiologist comes into the room, you really welcome him as the Messiah. I think you could promise him anything at that moment to make you feel better! It's amazing the feeling of gratitude you can conceive for this man, once he's administered it to you."

Peter has a slightly different view of this supposedly miraculous moment:

"The epidural my wife was given did not work well. When the doctor realized that it was only working on half of her pelvis and back, there was nothing more he could do. The labor was going on, the child was coming out. We had to move on. As a result, the mother-to-be felt all the contractions on one side and not on the other. "It's better than no epidural at all, but it wasn't nirvana! What I saw that day made me realize that it wasn't a sham at all: Aurelie really looked like she was in pain. I don't wish any woman not to be able to use this method", concludes the husband, still shocked by the spectacle.

"Our mothers and grandmothers were all heroines," said a friend of mine, who has been a mother for barely a month. What about all the others on the planet who are not lucky enough to give birth in hospitals that offer epidurals?

This first pain, almost common to all women, is coupled with other fears associated with barbaric names: "forceps", "suction cup", "episiotomy". The complications that follow childbirth also give rise to many fantasies in the imagination of future parents and all those who will never be parents. A midwife testifies that things have improved over the last few years.

"When I was a student, you could be sure that 100% of primiparous women had an episiotomy. All the doctors and midwives had their scissors on hand, ready to use. It didn't matter if the baby's head could finally go through on its own." Why?" It was considered better that way, so much so that in our internship we got no points if we delivered a primipara without having performed an episiotomy. So the midwives, in search of points for their degree, were cutting perineums all day!" And today? "We wait to see if the head will pass or not, if there is a risk that the perineum will tear, if we will use forceps or a suction cup, or if the baby presents badly (by the breech notably). Sometimes a simple manipulation is enough to guide the baby and turn him or her without needing to do more."

These unfriendly images that circulate, on the Internet or in the imagination, are enough to create an unhealthy and impressive climate around childbirth. It is therefore easier to understand the renunciation of some women, who are kept in this uncontrollable fear. Faced with the unknown which opens like an abyss, they move back, refusing to undergo "this butchery".

One of the causes of the lack of desire for motherhood is also the trauma passed on from generation to generation: if you look hard enough, you may find deaths related to childbirth. The time is not very far when women had a high probability of dying in childbirth. And this risk has not totally disappeared today.

For every 100,000 births in France, slightly more than 7 women die during pregnancy, childbirth or in the weeks following[40]. According to the Institut de veille sanitaire (INVS), which is a member of the National Expert Committee on Maternal Mortality (CNEMM), "the event can be considered rare." However, in the eyes of some women, the risk is not worth taking. Their fear acts as a self-defense reflex.

Contrary to the physical pain linked only to the contractions, the other forms of suffering, psychological this time, which concern everything that can go wrong during a birth, are generally kept silent. It is delicate to evoke these moments, to tell about this "delivery", which for these mothers, was

---

40. The maternal mortality ratio is the ratio of maternal deaths in a year to the number of live births in that year, usually expressed per 100,000.

not really a delivery. They pass on their experience almost ashamedly. In their memories choked with sorrow, remorse and regret, they mix physical and psychic pain. The sobs resurface, imprisoning the word. The remorse of not having been "able" to breastfeed their child as soon as it was born as they had planned, of not having been able to touch it, of having barely or not at all seen it because they themselves were in a worrying state. These are all cases that bind the memory, mortgaging the future mother-child relationship. Something has been missing since birth.

DEFINITION OF MATERNAL DEATH

Maternal death is "the death of a woman during pregnancy or within 42 days after its termination, regardless of its duration or location, from any cause determined or aggravated by the pregnancy or the care it prompted, but neither accidental nor fortuitous".

Maternal deaths fall into two groups:
1) "Deaths from direct obstetrical causes: these are those resulting from obstetrical complications (pregnancy, labor and delivery), interventions, omissions, incorrect treatment or a chain of events resulting from any of the above factors;
2) "Deaths by indirect obstetrical causes: these are those resulting from a pre-existing disease or condition that developed during pregnancy without being due to direct obstetrical causes, but which was aggravated by the physiological effects of pregnancy."

The risk of maternal death is highly correlated with age. It is **minimal between the ages of 20 and 24 and remains very low until 29**. It increases sharply from the age of 35, since it is **three times higher at 35-39 years of age** and twelve times higher at 45 years of age than at 20-24 years of age.

Distribution of maternal deaths by pathology.

During the period 1995-1997, **delivery or immediate postpartum hemorrhage was the leading cause, accounting for 12% of deaths**, eclampsia accounted for 8%, as did amniotic embolism for 8%, and pulmonary embolism for 7% of deaths; almost as frequent were antepartum hemorrhage or cesarean section without any other indication, each of which accounted for approximately 6% of causes of maternal death.
Maternal deaths due to other obstetric complications remain high, at 4% of deaths, despite a slight downward trend from previous years. Half of these deaths are the direct result of cesarean section.

NB: Studies provided by the Ministry of Health
http://www.sante.gouv.fr/htm/pointsur/maternite/rapport3.htm
Compulsory registration of births and all deaths in France is the regular source of information for studying maternal mortality and its causes in France. The National Institute of Statistics and Economic Studies (INSEE) and the National Institute of Health and Medical Research (Inserm-SC8) are the organizations responsible for compiling general mortality statistics.

How can one be happy when the birthday of the beloved child arrives, when this moment is definitely associated with a butchery difficult to forget? For some, celebrating the passing years is like celebrating a day that could have been the day of their own death. How to mourn without making the child feel it, nor to put a debt on his frail and innocent shoulders, a burden by definition too heavy for him?

In this part of my "quest-investigation", I go from one woman to another, this time rubbing shoulders with many mothers. I take in their pain, their joy, I wander between their ambiguities, reassured to see that they also have their own contradictions, like all women without children and just like me. Whether I choose to have children or not, I have to accept that I will never know everything, nor realize all my fantasies. If I remain a nulliparous woman, I will never know what it means to give life to a being of flesh and blood that is half my creation. I will only be able to imagine, without being sure to have really understood all the dimensions of this act. On the other hand, if I embark on the path of motherhood and parenthood, I won't know what it means to be childless at 40, 50, 60 and beyond. Around me, the looks become more severe: "Choose your side", I sometimes have the impression of hearing in my ear. The injunctions of some, the fears of others, the unpleasant and useless rumors slap me in turn.

I stop and try to think: "Don't, you haven't learned anything," says an ultra-converted mother, "you mustn't think, you must let yourself be carried along and act." Act? Translate this verb by "to make a child". My grandmother, an ardent protector of the maternal cause, tells me often enough:

- Women of your generation, you are too much in the wait-and-see, in the in-between. By hoping for a sign from heaven, you will get nothing at all and you will miss the most important and wonderful thing for a woman!

- But you, grandma, you didn't suffer, you weren't afraid to give birth alone?

- Pain? Everyone has pain somewhere, you don't get anything for nothing, and then you forget about it. Perfection does not exist, or if it does, in your head, it is up to you to create it, to invent it!

My grandmother never feels sorry for herself. Until the day one of my best friends became pregnant. My grandmother smiled and regularly checked on her friend, giving me tender looks, winks and side comments.

"You too, my dear, it will happen to you one day, your turn will come!"

Did I ask her to reassure me about my "condition", to tell me if my turn was coming? I turn my tongue seven times in my mouth and answer nothing. When the birth arrives and my grandmother asks me how the child's arrival went, I tell her about my friend's misadventures in having an episiotomy. My grandmother suddenly puts on a serious face, becomes extremely sympathetic; I see her cracking her armor and pitying her, mixing in her own memories relegated behind a panel of memory that she had not lifted in half a century. Her three children are over fifty years old and the memory of the pain is apparently still vivid.

- An episiotomy? It's more rare for a second child, she said. I was in so much pain, my granddaughter, I remember, I had to put on a brave face, I had no choice, but I had lost so much blood. I felt so tired, I thought it was normal, in reality I was completely anemic.
- Grandma, I thought it was easy...
- No, she says. Not easy: wonderful.

Chapter 5

Psychological reasons
for not wanting a child

"- And then Kiki, the dog, is quite enough to entertain us...

She was basically of the same opinion, she finally admitted to her husband: a dog was as much fun, and even much more fun than a child, and if she had considered having a child for a while, it was mostly out of conformity, and also to please her mother, but in reality she didn't really like children, she had never really liked them, And he didn't like children either, if he wanted to think about it, he didn't like their natural and systematic egoism, their original ignorance of the law, their fundamental immorality which forced an exhausting and almost always fruitless

education. No, children, in any case human
children, he decidedly did not like them."

Michel Houellebecq,
The Map and the Territory[41]

The selfish part: the refusal to become an adult or to take charge of someone other than oneself

"This weekend, I'm going to Eurodisney with three girl-friends, will you come with us?" a friend asks me. No, she's not playing babysitter, nor has she been forced to take care of a nephew or a niece who has been nagging her since Christmas because of a promise lost under the tree or declaimed at the end of a family meal to get rid of a too clingy gang. For her, this trip to the land of Mickey, Cinderella and Pocahontas is a delicious way to occupy her day. Three months later, when I ask her to come with me to a hammam, I hear myself answer: "Sorry, but I already booked my day to go to the Japan Expo in Villepinte." Translate: a huge gathering of Japanese manga and video game fans, most of whom will go dressed as their favorite character.

Let's be honest: if I scrutinize my habits as a young thirty-something, I will find one or two proofs of absolute regression. But these will not determine our desire to have children or not, nor the possibility of educating children smaller than

---

41. HOUELLEBECQ (Michel), *La Carte et le Territoire*, Flammarion, Paris, 2010, 432 p.

ourselves. Should we inevitably be ultra-serious to become parents? Do we have to say no to parties that go on until 7 a.m., to curb our retarded teenage desires? No. However, in the long run, these habits don't sit well with small, defenseless beings who are in need of rules, sleep and a caring and attentive presence.

Among the people I have met, many have dropped the word "selfishness" without much trouble. There is no question of detecting narcissism or a total insensitivity to the fate of the children around them. What resounds more is the playful and voluntarily disorganized aspect of a life that refuses to fit into "bourgeois" codes. Thus, Joshua, who works in institutional communication, begins with this confession.

"I must admit that one of the reasons why I don't want to become a father is because I am selfish. I have a very pleasant life, I do what I want, when I want, I do not want to put an insoluble problem on my back. For me, a child is the equivalent of an open-ended contract, but with the added bonus of a lot of trouble. You know when it starts, but you don't know when it will stop.

He talks about children as a prison sentence:

"You're looking at twenty years minimum."

Is it a coincidence that among those who have given me a similar speech, I find mainly men on the one hand and single people on the other? Not that these men do not share the life and heart of someone, but it is clear that few of them officially commit themselves to a couple life, to marriage or

Psychological reasons for not wanting a child

even to cohabitation. Jacques, a dashing 50-year-old, is part of this family of hardened bachelors who are afraid of the word "family". Spending Christmas with his brothers and sisters and their offspring? A nightmare. To be immersed in a wedding with two hundred guests, of whom he would only know 5%? A horror he has firmly and definitively decided to do without.

"It's simple, I refuse everything and I never justify myself," he says. For thirty years, his way of life has been a mystery to his family; he regularly gives news of himself, accepts to take a train to visit his parents who then welcome him like the prodigal son, authorizes others to talk about his work, but never extends himself on his private life.

Having a child also means giving up a certain amount of laziness and indolence and being organized in a way that reduces the time spent on pleasurable activities.

In general, what happens if I forget to send a health form to Social Security, order a new checkbook, gather the information needed to renew my press card, or follow up with the accounting department of a newspaper that forgot to pay my freelance fees? I lose money. Stupidly. What is the immediate penalty if I miss the deadline to send in my tax return or pay my rent? I inevitably face derogatory remarks, as well as a surcharge. The consequence is once again financial.

Let's imagine the same scene with a child: can a mother forget to register her child at the nursery school, miss the date of the pre-school meeting, confuse the tennis class with the drawing class of her offspring, forget to send the check for the school lunch, make a mistake in the day or time of the pediatrician's appointment, not have done the shopping and end up with a fridge that is three quarters empty, without diapers or milk on a public holiday? Between the permanent guilt that already assails me, just by thinking about it, and the vision of the organization worthy of a chief of staff that I will have to adopt, my nerves give out, my pulse accelerates and my heart beats not the chamade, but the recall of the troops. Everything in me screams "help".

The organization of new parents can rightly be frightening: the days remain the same number of hours, but you have to do twice as much and manage to find time to take care of your child. There are two solutions: either you hire outside help (nanny, grandparents, daycare) or you reduce the amount of work you used to do. Even with excellent in-home help, family schedules no longer resemble those of single people or couples without children. Agreeing to go to dinner with friends, to a restaurant, to go on vacation, even for a weekend, means agreeing to ask for help, or to inconvenience those around you. Some people categorically refuse the idea.

The organization required for a child seems to me at best a waste of time, at worst exasperating," explains Stanislas. Asking for help from others has always seemed inconceivable to me. I don't like to ask for favors from my loved ones, I want to be self-sufficient, independent, self-reliant. However, I don't mind helping my loved ones, but I prefer to be the one who helps, rather than the one who needs help."

Psychological reasons for not wanting a child

Thus, this thirty-year-old ready to do anything to avoid becoming a father readily admitted that his 3-year-old nephew sincerely touched him:

"Of course, my nephew is extremely endearing, I love him very much, but taking care of him is a real full-time job. There is no break. I can't fit it into my own life. I know how to change a diaper and I've kept him before. I walk him sometimes, I spend time with him. I enjoy it even more because it's not mine and it's exceptional moments. No permanent responsibility."

A reaction that is not only found among anonymous people. Recently, during an interview where the journalist asked him if he envisaged his life with or without children, the Belgian comedian Benoît Poelvoorde answered: "It terrifies me to be responsible for someone. Already, being responsible for my dog, it scares me. Then, to communicate my anguish to my child! I would hate myself for that[42]..."

Antoine, who defines himself as "a kid", also admits that he is afraid of the task: "It's the long-term responsibility that a child implies that seems too heavy to me. However, when he talks about his relationship with the children, we can guess a beautiful complicity:

"In the United States, I was an instructor. I wasn't strict with them, I played, I was always clowning around. They heckled me a lot and knew that with me, it was a party. If I were a father, how would I react and behave? My wife is a cartoon character herself, we are good together because we

---

42. *In Télérama* n° 3181, of December 29, 2010, p. 34.

don't take ourselves seriously. But we certainly wouldn't know how to behave as responsible parents."

First, find your place in society

I think about Victor, his trajectory resembles those of many young people who, after leaving college, have not yet really found their path or aspire to other paths than those of their parents. He sails from one small job to another, from one mission to another, rocking like a boat drunk with adventure, in search of a vocation and meaning.

"Why not have a child? That's such a premature question! More globally, I haven't yet identified a more important issue for me: how to find my place in today's society. When I have found that, I will be more able to ask myself the question of having children or not."

On the eve of his 30th birthday, Victor still has time to find his way and provide one or more answers to his question. Will he then be tempted to commit to parenthood? Will he want to reproduce, once he feels in tune with himself and has made his nest in our vast world?

At fifty-something, Sonia answered. She too had been searching for her path for a long time. Digging her way meant first of all knowing where she came from: a difficult task, given the convoluted history of her family, parents, grandparents and forefathers.

Psychological reasons for not wanting a child

"I succeeded in tracing my family tree during a long psychoanalytical work undertaken to understand why I always went towards "forbidden" men, that is to say, men already taken. My love affairs were almost always impossible. I also wanted to know why my sister and I had no desire for a child."

The story she uncovered dates back to the early nineteenth century, when her great-great-grandmother was in the service of a count. The count's son fell in love with her and they had a secret affair, from which two illegitimate children were born.

"When the first one was born, she was chased out of the house, because at that time, a son of a good family, moreover an aristocrat, did not marry a servant. In spite of this, their father always remained present. Financially, he helped her, especially with the education of his sons."

Later, this woman married a man who gave her his family name, the one that Sonia currently bears with her brother and sister. And then, extraordinarily, history repeats itself, again in the form of a nose-thumbing at social conventions:

"His eldest daughter, my great-grandmother, had a son out of wedlock: my future grandfather. He will carry the family name of his mother, which explains the transmission of our patronymic by women. By reaction who knows, my grandfather married an extremely prudish woman. Together they had only one son: my father. He would not risk having a daughter, he did not want them, as they were sinners, embodying the fault and bastardy.

This intergenerational secret of natural children has stamped love with the seal of the forbidden: "I inherited this role of woman who must keep silent, hide, conceal a heavy secret", Sonia soberly and placidly analyzes.

If she wants to tell me her genealogy and if I want to tell it here, it is because the events that preceded Sonia's birth weighed heavily in her choice: to privilege the family business to the detriment of her private life and her future motherhood. Let's listen to her again.

"We are bourgeois artisans. My father was raised by an English nanny. My grandfather was the head of a workshop specializing in fine jewelry, goldsmithing and gilding, while my uncle worked in gilding. My father, the child of such a puritanical couple, had become a runner! He loved women like his grandfather before him. One year after meeting my father, my mother Andrée was already a cuckold. Eight years separate my brother and me, I always wonder what happened during that time. Why did she wait so long? When she had me, she was unhappy, but I know that I was a real sponge.

At the age when one takes charge of one's life, that is to say at the threshold of one's studies, Sonia decides to go into business while her youngest daughter lets her artistic sensibility speak and becomes a jewelry designer. She is about to start her own career, which should have taken her far away from the family business, when a major and disastrous event occurs, upsetting everything in its path:

"I was 25 years old when my father passed away. I had a degree in technology and marketing, I should have gone to Procter & Gamble at that time, and then the question of taking over the family business became crucial. If I didn't take

Psychological reasons for not wanting a child

it over, it would have been sold or declared bankrupt. I rolled up my sleeves and decided to take over my father's business. I learned everything on the job."

Suddenly, at the age of 40, the first awakening, the first shock:

"I thought to myself, 'oh lala, you can't go through life without experiencing a truly great love story!"

Her reflex? She keeps turning to the same profile of men: aesthetes, with strong personalities, pleasure seekers, fascinating and very interesting intellectually, but unfaithful. Then, in 2007, she made a decision that had far-reaching consequences: she sold the family business because she had finally found who she was and what she was made for. She was then 46 years old.

"My decision was made in September 2004, it was an act of liberation, I cut the cord, I finally took my independence from my father and my family heritage.

The sale of the company freed her from a weight and opened other doors. She finally allowed herself to love a man who is not "forbidden", without a second life or hidden part.

"Today, I love a man who is eleven years older than me. With him, I feel like a teenager in the sense that he plays the role of protector, without being too much so. I was looking for Love with a capital L, I finally found it. Children are the story of another life or the story of my friends.

The refusal to pass on one's faults:
the management of violence

At the origin of the refusal to transmit, I have encountered in several cases a fear, even a fear: that of reproducing a family model associated with failure. In the eyes of the people concerned, "perpetuating oneself" only means transmitting one's own defects. It is therefore understandable that heredity is a frightening fact. And for good reason.

Among those I interviewed, some had had violent parents. This violence is not always physical, it could be psychological (divorce is a form of violence, the unspoken and the taboos are another) and it could have done as much damage. It can be verbal, repetitive or occasional. Another form of violence, often repressed, is the one directly linked to my subject of investigation: the desire for a child. Adults may have felt, without formally knowing it, that they were not wanted. The evil has insinuated itself in them little by little, without anyone, including themselves, being aware of it. One of the direct consequences of this work of the unconscious is that they will not have any desire to repeat what their parents inflicted on them. When the process has been completed in the light of day and the unconscious has emerged, this decision can be made more serenely, but when it is based on objective ignorance, the evil continues to do damage. It is then very complicated to "heal one's inner child", according to the beautiful expression of Moussa Nabati[43].

---

43. NABATI (Moussa), *Guérir son enfant intérieur*, LGF, coll. Le Livre de Poche, Paris, 2009.

"The identity is paradoxically double. The 'house-itself' with the image of a Russian doll or gigogne, is thus not exclusively inhabited by only one tenant, the famous 'I', conscious, lucid, realistic, desiring, acting, reasonable and reasoning, subjected to the principle of reality, as Descartes conceived and described it so well. It shelters at least a second guest, invisible this one, although master on board, namely the inner child, the little boy or girl that each one was, that he is still today and that he will always remain, beyond his sex, his social position and especially his age. The past does not fade away. It will never disappear, and fortunately so, insofar as it represents the roots of the being, its foundations, the source and the reservoir, for all life, of its vital energy, its inspiration and its creativity! [...] Thus, every being shelters in him two egos, two Selves, two realms, two sensibilities, two visions of oneself, of life, of the world and of the others; every being is bipolar, bilateral, two-headed, bilingual. [...] The adult Ego represents certainly the emerged part of the iceberg, the authority and the seat of the conscience, the judgment, the will and the action. It assumes, like the captain of a ship, the function of mediator between the claims of the drives, the imperatives of the superego and the requirements of the external reality. [...] But he also risks, in case of conflict, to see himself submerged, influenced, mistreated, held on a leash, by the occult power of his inner child, of which he is not aware and which he fails, consequently, to master. In these conditions, the strength or the weakness of the adult Ego, the good or the bad image that it has of itself, its combativeness or its softness, its temerity or its cowardice depend on the state of health of the inner child, its solidity or its fragility. It is in fact the latter that guides the steps of the former towards joyful appointments or precipitates them, on the contrary, into the throes of worries and sadomasochistic codependencies, despite the intelligence and the will of the "adult". When this one is under the unconscious influence of his inner child, he ceases precisely to feel and react as an adult. He becomes blind, losing his psychic autonomy."

A little further on in his book, Moussa Nabati points out that the inner child has "two facets, dark or bright, depending on what he has integrated from his family and transgenerational past, what he has undergone or experienced, what he has succeeded or failed to overcome[44]."

This point, in the case of a child who was not wanted, is essential. Two questions then arise: first, has the adult child become explicitly aware of his or her accidental origin (his or her parents have admitted it to him or her, thus beginning his or her resilience work), or does he or she only sense it through details, sibylline phrases? Secondly, has he had the opportunity to discuss it with family members, third parties, friends, a psychologist or a psychotherapist, or has he placed a leaden blanket over the subject, locking it up and turning it into a heavy and suffocating taboo?

---

44. *Ibid*, p. 20.

To illustrate these issues, here are two cases that are interesting to compare, because, although they have something in common (being unwanted children), they are opposite each other in the way they deal with their past.

Hervé and Anaïs both have a childhood marked by the DDASS; Anaïs directly, Hervé indirectly, via his parents. However, Hervé himself describes his family as "strange":

"There are only three of us," he explains, "my mother, my older sister who is 33 years old and me; my father died in 1999. My parents were both children of the DDASS. I didn't find out until very late. They met when they were about 15 years old, at the DDASS, because neither of them had a foster family. Together we did some research to find out if my potential grandparents were alive, but we found nothing. Maybe I have cousins and relatives elsewhere, but I don't know."

Today, Hervé lives in Chile, thousands of miles away from his mother and sister, and has no children. At 38 years old, one might say, there is no hurry, especially for a man, but he himself is almost convinced that he will never have any. He doesn't want any and has always been very clear about this with his partners. For more than six years he has been sharing the life of Clara, a journalist he met in France during one of his returns to the country between two trips.

"I had to spend a few months in France to settle some business. I didn't hide my intention to go back to Chile, and she offered to follow me. Honestly, at first, I didn't believe it! I've already heard this version so many times at parties where we remake the world, I no longer count the number

No Children. It Makes Sense!

of friends telling me that they were going to leave everything to go abroad, remake their lives, etc. In the end, they don't do it. Clara asked me to wait for her, while she prepared her departure too, putting an end to her work, and then she joined me. Our cohabitation was not easy, because I had opened my bar while she hardly spoke a word of Spanish and I had to translate everything for her. I had enough. I told her to go on her own tour of Latin America, to live her life, to discover the countries and find her own way. Then we would see. She came back a year later, spoke perfect Spanish and we decided to start our business, a travel agency."

In the case of Anaïs, everything is extremely painful and complicated. If the unspoken words dominated her life for years, she succeeded in extracting herself from her childhood and decided to testify for all those who find themselves or have found themselves in a similar situation.

Anaïs is one of three children; each of them will be successively "abandoned" by their mother who, too young and too fragile, feels unable to take care of them. Nevertheless, she did not separate herself from them in a permanent way, but for more or less long periods of time, necessary, according to her, to build an image of mother. Today, Anaïs who is about fifty years old, affirms that her past "is washed away".

"It's clarity. I'm 54 years old, I don't have children and I don't regret it, because I know why and I accept myself as I am. Socially, I have never been disturbed by it, because let's not forget that I belong to the 'pill generation'. At my age,

Psychological reasons for not wanting a child

many women have made this choice not to procreate and I don't feel like a special case, a kind of alien. I have friends who are mothers and others who are not."

It was not socially that Anaïs had to accept herself, but psychologically. Her victory opened the way to resilience: understanding why she didn't want to have children, why she didn't even think about it. She found the answer in a devastated childhood. In addition to the abandonment of her mother as a young girl, she was a victim of incest.

"Around 30, when it was my turn to think about children, I realized that I didn't want any," she says.

Years go by, she does not change her mind. No desire to create a family where she would be the anchor, she does not feel comfortable with that.

"It took me a long time to realize that I had no place for a child, because my inner child was broken," she says in a soft voice.

When she begins to understand the importance of childhood on her life, she decides to search her past. She then starts to investigate: to know, to raise parts of her blocked memory, to reappropriate her inner child and to reconcile with herself. Before this ultimate step, she had to dig up all the weeds, feeling what was toxic around her.

"During this investigation, I unfortunately uncovered another incest. A generation before me, my aunt (let's call her Rosie) was also sexually abused." It turns out that the man guilty of molesting her aunt is the same man who molested her. A member of the family, but who does not have a blood link with the two women, it is a "patch": Rosie's stepfather (the second husband of her mother). Anaïs has always refused to name him and refers to him as "the Stranger". When he turns around the young Anaïs, Rosie is no longer there. For obscure and mysterious reasons (or perceived as such at the time by the whole family), she has cut ties with everyone, her mother, her brothers and sister. She is therefore not present to protect her niece by unmasking the Stranger. I can't help but wonder if anyone in the family circle knew. Could Rosie's mother not know what her husband had done to her daughter? Could she still be unaware when her husband does it again years later to one of her granddaughters? A gigantic taboo was created around this abuse of which were victims, on two successive generations, two girls. Coincidence? Neither of these two women will have children. Neither of them will get married.

The same cause has the same consequences. Each had her inner child broken, preventing her from giving birth and caring for another child. At the end of her investigation, Anaïs saw her aunt again, the latter had not gone very far. Her own family must not have pushed their investigations very far. What about their desire to know what had happened to her? Did the family members know? Were they afraid of digging up something sordid that they would rather not see come to the surface? Did the disappearance of the ugly duckling, the one who had suffered the irreparable, suit everyone, placing them in a *status quo* that, if not clear, was safe?

Is there an older chain, have other women in the family also been abused? By going back up the family tree, Anaïs will

Psychological reasons for not wanting a child

bring to light another single woman left without children. She won't get more details on why and how, but the fact is there. This repetition is strange or on the contrary "speaking", three generations have had their "old girl"! Horrible expression to designate those whom the society has difficulty in integrating into its traditional schemes. Society prefers to judge and classify these women, rather than trying to understand the reasons for their choice and, inevitably, to ask more refined questions. These women are victims that their own families treat as guilty.

Anaïs will only start to lie on the couch after the death of her father, and after having carried out her satellite work, i.e. the family investigation, preliminary to all the rest. Her psychoanalytical work will begin at a close frequency, at a rate of three sessions per week during four years. She learned to put words to her recovered memory and to weave the thread of the family pattern that led to her. Her mother was an orphan, a child of the DDASS, while her paternal grandfather abandoned son and wife. Anaïs has the impression that the toxicity is inscribed in the family unconscious and that she will not be able to get rid of it. How, under these conditions, can she give birth to children herself, become a mother, without abandoning them one day in her turn? Two solutions: not to procreate, or to evacuate the fear of predestination, of a *fatum*. When she leaves her psychoanalysis, Anaïs is already more than 45 years old.

"It was too late to consider being a mother. Besides, I still didn't want to, but this time it wasn't out of fear or ignorance."

She thought about it, cleared it and then cleaned it up. She let go, and at the same time got rid of her inferiority complex.

"After being permanently insecure, I made the mothers around me insecure. My sister-in-law, my brother's wife, didn't accept me well, she was afraid I would steal her sons."

What a shame! It was necessary for her to overcome the *ego* and to cut down the rotten tree that was lodged in her.

Let's go back to Hervé for a moment. Contrary to Anaïs, he does not want to see a corollary between his childhood, the history of his parents, children of the DDASS, and his choice not to want a child:

"I don't think that story influenced me. I'm not really into psychology. My mother, it weighs on her: my sister still doesn't have a child and has trouble settling down with someone. I'm the last one to bear my father's name, I don't give a damn; my mother does. There was no one before her, there will be no one after me."

I would now like to talk about Victor who is younger than Hervé, but who has a similar background. They both share the same way of conceiving life, of wanting to find a personal balance: they are looking for their way. Their parents' divorce is not insignificant in their lives. However, where Hervé refuses to enter into an analysis and to take the time to understand the reasons which push him to not want children, Victor confided to me to try to "analyze" his journey.

"I come from a divorced family, and I don't want to reproduce this model, nor to impose it on a child. My

Psychological reasons for not wanting a child

parents, moreover, divorced very late, certainly too late, only eight years ago, after having lived together for twenty-five years. I saw them fighting, quarrelling, hating each other during my childhood and adolescence. It's not a happy, optimistic sight for a child. It was a bit rough, I could hear them arguing, sometimes I would catch snippets of conversation. Apparently, my older sister was not expected, she was not necessarily wanted, then my parents stayed together to assume. All this came out. I probably have an unconscious trauma with this. Since then, I run away from conflicts. Today, I try to go deeper, I want to understand."

Finally, let us recall another testimony, that of Stanislas, the lawyer from Nice who is a supporter of vasectomy. He explained to me that he did not want a child because his girlfriend forgot to take the pill when he was 19 years old.

Throughout our conversation, however, he failed to mention a very important point (which he would eventually drop when I asked him what his parents thought of his decision): his mother's death. The event is stated almost in spite of himself, at the end of our conversation. He would like to give the impression that this tragedy is not directly related to his current position on children. To love is to become attached, and to become attached is to risk losing this person who is tenderly attached to you, and therefore to open a door to suffering, to expose yourself dangerously. Without even mentioning the risk of betrayal. Two sources of pain from which Stanislas protects himself by refusing to get involved in a long, honest, balanced relationship.

The relationship with the mother and the father

Refusing to have children, to transmit and to inscribe one's history in a lineage, is also refusing to do as one's mother or father. In this case, the message in the process of identification with the mother for girls, and with the father for boys, is very clear: "There is no question of living like her/him!"

The family transmission of rules and codes, conscious or unconscious, from one generation to another, especially from mother to daughter, seems to me to be very significant in the decision of young women to have a child or not. Even if, as I wrote at the beginning of this book, the intentions expressed are rarely in line with future behavior (about 4% of couples will never actually have a child, this is a constant in Europe). Why do women, especially younger women, express the wish not to have children? Behind this wish lies the desire not to reproduce a family pattern. According to Anaïs, "it's all about the relationship with the mother. How was the link with her built?" This is the central question for this psychotherapist.

CEO of a company, Françoise works in finance, an environment usually dominated by men. For a long time, she lived between Europe and Asia, spending her time traveling, working more than fifteen hours a day and taking a minimum of vacations, except when she leaves for a month or two to cut her ties with her world. She travels by foot, bus and train, quenching her thirst for discovery in Laos, Cambodia, Indonesia, stopping in Bali to relax, or in China. Françoise comes from an ultra-traditional, rigorous family. She has seven brothers and sisters.

"My mother always made it clear to my sisters and me that our only goal was to get married as soon as possible. When I say quickly, that could be as early as 18, which is not uncommon in my family, and of course without having had sex before marriage. Our destiny was then to have in turn six, seven, eight children."

To this rigid education, the traces of which are still visible years later, was added a lack of emotional involvement on the part of his parents, which today explains his choice not to have a child:

"On the one hand, we were not allowed to go out, but on the other hand, we were not allowed to bring friends home either. We had to justify all our comings and goings all the time. When I was about 20 years old, I had a lover, a very presentable boy who my parents liked because he fit their criteria. I almost married him and went down the path that my mother had laid out for me since I was a child. At the last moment, I changed my mind, I explained calmly to this boy, who didn't hold it against me, that this path was not for me. I realized that I had other ambitions and that I didn't want to reproduce the family pattern or make my own children suffer as I had suffered.

Another confession, another story. Laurene, too, throws me as if in echo: "This discussion about the desire for motherhood has an obvious link to the mother, and mine is not very serene."

Laurène has experienced some pretty strong and unusual events in her family unit.

"I have a wonderful mother, but she is very sick. She is in the hospital. When I was conceived, my parents were about to get divorced, and I don't think my mother could bear the thought of divorce. My parents are the opposite of each other in every way, even physically. My mother comes from a traditional, close-knit family, and my father from a family that looks like nothing, unable to express any feelings. I have always lived as a sort of joint between the two; I mended them. I discovered over time that my parents loved each other in their own way, but sincerely. My father decided to stay and they raised me together."

Laurène quickly appears to me divided between an immense admiration and gratitude towards the one who took care of her, and the will not to repeat the same pattern, not to sacrifice, like her mother, her artistic vocation on the altar of motherhood.

"I grew up with a not-so-happy mom, who kept going through ups and downs. She only went back to work when I was 8 years old because my father demanded that she take care of me. When I think back, she still devoted eight years of her life to me! She was an art teacher, but then she was humiliated in her job and fell into a deep depression. From then

Psychological reasons for not wanting a child

on, she went through cycles. For my father, it was difficult to bear. Despite this rough period, I always knew that she loved me. Her suicide attempts or accidents were messages to get our attention. Her first message she threw at my conception: "Stay there!" she seemed to say. Years later, the second was obviously meant for my father, when she fell down the stairs and broke her collarbone. From that point on, I became my mother's mother."

Repeat her mother's fate and find herself in the condition of a married woman, in love, mother of a family and prisoner? This was out of the question for Laurène, who chose a different path than that of self-pity and despair. She decided very quickly that no man would bully her, nor force her to put the brakes on her career. From the United States to Japan, via London and Italy, she has drawn inspiration, studied the fine arts of many cultures, learned languages, rubbed shoulders with different lifestyles, observed, listened. Her learning path has doubled as a self-analysis. To heal oneself is to learn to know oneself; to learn is to heal... and to heal.

Jennifer could echo Laurène's words. Her lack of desire for a child, she tells me, "is surely due to [her] family situation," which is very complex. She concedes with a smile that she had "a rather eventful childhood". We'll see that this is still less than the truth. To begin with, Jennifer was not raised by her mother, but by her grandmother.

"I am an only child," she says. "My maternal grandparents took me in almost at birth and kept me until I was 4 years old. At the time, my mother visited me regularly, as she lived in the same town as us, in the Paris region."

The reasons her mother abandoned her are not extremely clear: her age - when she got pregnant she was "15" and "16 when I was born". According to Jennifer, the major pitfall was that she was not cut out to be a mother. Despite this, the young woman still sincerely believes that her mother loved her, even though "she shouldn't have had me. She wanted to live her life, to have fun." Later, when she was only 4 years old, her grandmother became ill: "My mother took me in. At the time, she was still living with my father. Two years later, they separated, in a very violent way. One night, my father threw us out of the house, he really threw us in the street, I was 6 years old. My grandmother took me back under her roof while my mother went to look for work in another city." After this traumatic episode for the little girl, her father, far from repenting, gave hardly any sign of life. He never went back on this sharing of tasks (from which he had been absent since her birth, since it had always been an arrangement between the mother and the grandparents), and never asked for custody of his daughter or even to take her from time to time on weekends or during vacations. "He was satisfied with this unspoken 'agreement'." Her grandparents then considered Jennifer as their second daughter and educated her as such: "This forced my grandfather, who was retired, to move around. Before me, they had had four children and my mother was their youngest."

As a teenager, things start to turn around. The wheels of life turned. "I had to take care of my grandmother who had

Psychological reasons for not wanting a child

health problems. This probably explains why I didn't have a teenage crisis at that time - it would come later, around age 26, when I got my driver's license. I must say that my aunts didn't lift a finger to help us. They thought it was very convenient that I was there. At the same time, my grandmother had taken such good care of me that I thought it was only fair. I never considered it an obligation to take care of my grandparents. My grandfather passed away when I was 13. With my grandmother, we became very close.

At no point does her mother offer to take Jennifer back with her. Yet she found work and started living with her husband again. Despite all this, Jennifer says she is satisfied: "I saw her every two weeks, which suited us both. I preferred to live with my grandmother because I didn't get along with my stepfather very well.

As the years go by, the girl becomes a young woman and her appetites evolve too.

"When I got my driver's license, a new horizon opened up for me. I started to go out a lot, to see boys. My grandmother was extremely worried, she was afraid of what people would say, of how the neighbors would look at me, but also that I would fall in love and abandon her. In fact, she was afraid that I would reproduce the pattern I had been a victim of. We loved each other very much and she couldn't stand my independence. At 28, I finally decided to live alone. She passed away two months later. When she died, I felt very guilty.

What Jennifer didn't mention was that her mother had already passed away by then. "Luckily, she didn't have any other children besides me!" Since then, Jennifer is almost an orphan, having no contact with her father. Again, she tempers and swears that she "never had a problem with it!"

"My parents were not parents," she explains, "but they were in the biological sense, but that's it. They were in the biological sense, but that's it. When my mother died, my stepfather followed her a few months later. He couldn't bear to be without her. I was 16 years old at the time. My step-mother took a dislike to me, as the daughter of 'the other'. I constantly reminded her of my father's first wife. She couldn't stand it and asked my father not to take me. My father came to my grandmother's house and said, 'Either Jennifer comes to live with us and you will never see her again, or she stays with you and you will never hear from me again.' My grandmother didn't hesitate for a second, she kept me with her."

While Jennifer's childhood and adolescence were severely tested, she is not one of those people whose family history has devastated them. To me, she epitomizes the phenomenon of resilience that psychoanalyst Boris Cyrulnik holds dear. The conclusion is somewhere very simple: she was cherished and loved in abundance, even if not by her parents.

"My grandparents were very close, they gave me a lot of love."

This would have inspired her to have children of her own. "It could have inspired me to start my own family, but no! I don't feel like it."

Psychological reasons for not wanting a child

No child without the meeting of the perfect being

Desire is not the only driver or brake in the question of parenthood. If, for the majority of the people I interviewed, desire is a driving force, like Jennifer, for others, the dilemma is more about choosing a partner. Eternal Arlesian, a tree that hides the forest, or a real search on their part, left unfulfilled? It is very difficult to sort out the motivations displayed.

"The number one problem when you decide to have a child is the mother," says Jacques, my "single" 50-year-old. "As long as I haven't found the ideal mother, I won't embark on the adventure. In the opposite case, it's too catastrophic! When I see the damage done to some of my friends, I don't want to make the same mistake."

With Jacques, the notion of a couple is evanescent. It is not a condition *sine qua non* for having a child. "Since it is impossible to know how long I will stay with a woman, that is the mother of my eventual child, to know if the love we will share will last or not, that conditions the future from another angle. I don't want to enter into a sordid permanent war based on blackmail, touching on questions of custody, education, or alimony. I need to be sure that the woman who would have the care of my child fits my cultural and social criteria."

The conclusion is similar for Cedric, a 33-year-old engineer, recently separated after a long relationship:

"I don't feel the need to reproduce, unless I find an exceptional woman with whom I can change my mind. When

I was younger, I would certainly have made a good father, I still had a dose of optimism to believe in it. Having a child now? Frankly, not so much! I think that people in their forties or even thirties, who finally have children late in life to fulfill a narcissistic desire, are selfish. They want a little one that looks like them so they can show it off to everyone!"

He has had more than enough opportunities to become a father, but none of the women he has lived with have been able to make him take the leap. His love profile? More faithful and attached than Don Juan at heart. He thus remained eight years with Véronique, his last companion. After their meeting in a city of the South of France and having lived there several years, Cedric expressed the desire to reconvert professionally; he then proposed to his companion to move on the Parisian area in order to be able to take again his studies.

"I was stagnating in my job, and I wanted to reach better positions, to become an executive. Véronique, who is a teacher, followed me without really being convinced by this move. I think she already wanted a child at that time, she thought that maybe I would agree once I had found a job that I would really enjoy and that would make me blossom."

As for Cédric, he has no intention of becoming a father. On the contrary, he wants to change his life, take risks and his diploma gives him wings.

"We supported each other at first. We were both happy not to have children. Little by little, each of us started to look in a different direction. I wanted more, I discovered I was ambitious and I wanted to train again to become an

Psychological reasons for not wanting a child

executive. For her part, she needed me to be her driving force, she was looking for someone to give her confidence. She was afraid of being a single mother. We probably would have been good parents, but only on the surface. We would have tried to get along. That's all. I didn't get along very well with my in-laws and there was a little bit of pressure, especially from them. My girlfriend was the eldest, her parents dreamed of being grandparents soon. They resented me, I think, because they thought I was a negative influence on their daughter in that respect. If she had been with a guy who had wanted to be a father, no doubt she would have jumped at it. To project with a woman, I need to share many commonalities with her, culturally, socially."

Men are not the only ones to look for the perfect man and to distinguish themselves by this quest. Women have told me that they are waiting for the ideal man, who has never come. Suzanne, an executive assistant in an international tax firm, is one of them.

"I didn't meet the man I was waiting for or who would have made me want to have a child. In my eyes, it is a couple project, I never considered it like some women who, around 40 years old, decide to have a child alone. I find that very selfish."

However, Suzanne's journey is quite classic at the beginning. When she was 15, she thought "like 80% of women" that she would have a child.

"I left school at a very young age, 16, and learned everything on the job. I'm pretty resourceful! My dream has always been to fly on my own, it's hard to share your space, to make room for a child. I went up to Paris and started training as a secretary. After my diploma, I went to England to be an au pair. I stayed there for two years and came back bilingual. Then nothing went as planned. When I was 26, I had my first abortion because I was pregnant by a man I didn't want to be with. The abortion took place at the Saint-Vincent-de-Paul hospital, and an anesthetist helped me. I was taking both the pill and antidepressants[45]."

Indecision

As we have seen in the previous chapters, the decision not to have children is rarely made on the spur of the moment. On the contrary, it is the result of a long process, and consequently, subject to the hazards of life. It is more or less firm depending on the person. It also happens that some women and men realize that they don't want a child until after twenty years. They never verbalized it, but always managed not to have any. The unconscious has made its way.

The late awakenings are then interpreted as an afterthought: "I didn't have a child, it's not a coincidence."

Cedric's journey describes quite well this permanent indecision which flirts, at first dilettante and then much more

---

45. The risk of becoming pregnant in this case is minimal, but it does exist; it affects about 2% of women.

Psychological reasons for not wanting a child

seriously, with the non-desire of a child. Although he still has many years ahead of him to change his mind, he feels convinced that he will never have a child.

"I have my own bubble that I like. I feel like the older I get, the more I put off having kids one day! I like to move, but with kids it seems hard. I wanted to go to Canada, but my girlfriend didn't want to go with me, so we split the difference and chose Paris. It was a mistake for both of us. She was not happy to have left the south and I felt frustrated not to have tried the great adventure across the Atlantic. Life with kids in the suburbs doesn't appeal to me at all, in which case I'd rather move back down south. But right now, I love my life here. I love the freedom that my job gives me and the opportunities to move up. My job gives me a certain comfort, it's nice, not only from a financial point of view, but also because I work with interesting people. At the same time, I also do theater, I have been acting since I was 9 years old. In retrospect, I realize that I never really left room for the possibility of having children. I always saw myself without. I never projected myself with children."

We continue to discuss his trajectory. He tells me that my request for an interview forced him to analyze his motivations and decisions. His view of couples with children is not negative, but he concludes that his turn has passed. For him, it is already too late.

"In a way, those who were right were those who had children early, around 20 years old. Thirteen, fourteen years later, they already have teenagers with them, it's not the same constraint. At 20, you don't think about it, it's innate, you feel like it, it's a matter of emotion. At my age, I'm more into reasoning. I think a lot about the consequences this would have on my future life. Children would jeopardize my independence. I want to do ten thousand things, I practice French boxing, savate. In a few years, I would like to start my own company, to be independent. The family is a constraint! I like to go out, to have a full social and emotional life. At the moment, I am single, but it is temporary. Being alone doesn't scare me. I know I will be able to experience something strong again with a girl."

Scanning his last fifteen years, since his own adolescence, he finds it necessary to tell me about his first experience of life in a couple.

"When I was 19 years old, I was captivated by a girl with whom I stayed for a long time. She was my first great love and even today I think of her with tenderness and nostalgia. She was the oldest of seven brothers and sisters. At that age, it's funny, I loved kids, and having five didn't scare me. With her, I was convinced that it would be a success, I mean even if later we had to separate. I knew by instinct that she would have been a good mother, that she would have taken care of them the way I wanted. Genetically too, I had a feeling that our children would have been beautiful and intelligent."

So, what is the reason that made him change his mind over time?

"I don't know, I discovered that life was more compli-cated, that having children was a huge responsibility. I took

Psychological reasons for not wanting a child

the measure of this madness! If I had to have children, it would have been with her. Since it didn't happen in the end, I probably won't have any with anyone else."

Finally, when I ask him how his indecision is translated and perceived by those around him, Cedric appears very placid and serene.

"My parents have stopped asking me about it. I have a brother who already has two children, so they are happy as grandparents. They loved my ex, Veronique, and they understood our life as a childless couple. At the same time, I'm sure my mom thinks I'll end up having them."

Let's take Anne who, in my survey, is a bit of an outsider. Indeed, she did not have a child, but she would have liked to. As a gynecologist, she had many options for recourse. However, curiously, she only tried *in vitro* fertilization once. Why did she give up everything? Today, married to another man, who also did not have a child, she does not regret anything, because she was able to look back on her past, to assess her desire for a child, which was ultimately ambivalent, and to explain her decisions.

"I had an imposed path. When I couldn't get pregnant naturally, I did an *in vitro* fertilization at the age of 34, which was the first and last one. My husband was not involved, he was macho and very proud and did not want to imagine that the fertility problem could come from him. He left me alone with this desire for a child, never questioning himself. However, in my eyes, having a child is a couple's project.

Both must be involved. He did not want to give of himself. I took advantage of a laparoscopy[46] to do my IVF. I had an embryo and then it left, I never knew what happened to it. The hormonal conditions were not right. Today I think that my infertility is due to a failure of my couple. Unconsciously, my child problem was an adult problem. Then I didn't think about it anymore. I didn't want to make any more attempts at assisted fertilization, my husband and I were living next door to each other. Despite this, I stayed with him for a long time, until I was 45, when we were already not getting along. When I was 35, I realized that I would never have a child with him. But I stayed. This logically mortgaged my probability of having one or more children in the future.

Anne tries to understand why she stayed with a man she knew she would never have children with. Was it out of fear of the future, fear of being alone, or because her life at that time was not so bad? Was her desire for a child willing to justify a whole range of sacrifices?

"I was living a free and very independent life. Maybe, after all, motherhood wasn't my thing. My desire for children was not so strong that I could consider it alone. It was never a question of satisfying my maternal fibre in my corner."

Françoise expressed herself freely for the first time on the subject of not wanting a child. It is the first time that she does not feel judged and that she can explain her choice, her

---

46. Final exploration of the fallopian tubes in the assessment of infertility.

Psychological reasons for not wanting a child

journey, without having to suffer the wrath of an audience or the reproaches of someone she is talking to. "It's a bit like going to the shrink," she says. I shudder. I'm not a psychologist, and I certainly don't pretend to be one, or to take the place of a therapist. In my heart, I begin to doubt the validity of my approach: what if she comes looking for answers, for help, that I am unable to provide? I don't want there to be any misunderstanding. I am here to listen, to receive her word, to question her. More strongly than the other women I have already met at this stage, she insists on anonymity. Her husband, Alain, is not aware of our interview.

She met him quite young, at 21 years old. The life she has led with him satisfies her. Through his words, I can guess a man with a strong personality who dominates her a little. Older than her, he had already been married once before meeting her. From this first union was born a son. "He had a child made behind his back," Françoise tells me. He does not ask for custody and sees him as little as possible, "once a month, the legal minimum". This son is a central element in Françoise's story, because he will condition her own life. Having the feeling of having been betrayed by his first wife, her husband will not take the same risks twice. For him, it is out of question to have another child. He wants to enjoy life without having to burden himself with a kid who will force him to save money, to arrange his schedule, to deprive himself in every sense of the word. When she met him, Françoise had just finished her studies and she liked the idea of working. She wants to take responsibility for herself and see what life has to offer. The idea of having a child never crossed her mind, she has no maternal instinct.

"Children in general like my husband immediately, I feel uncomfortable with them, I do not know how to deal with them, I do not know how to talk to them or play with a little one. I am not attracted."

At the age of 30, when some of her friends already had children, she bought a second home with Alain: a ruined building in Brittany. Everything had to be done. Restoring houses (they already own their own in the suburbs) is their great passion.

"Every weekend or so, we went there to do the work ourselves. It occupied our weekends and even our vacations for a long time. We were very proud. One day someone said to me, 'Lady, you put your fertility into construction.' I think that's totally true."

Once the house is finished, they begin a series of trips. Then came the fateful year of turning 40, "without my realizing it."

"Suddenly, I realized that if I wanted children, it was too late. Not that I wanted children, but I hadn't thought it through. I hadn't seen the years go by, nor had I taken the time to dig into the question. I had a hard time passing the 40th birthday, it was a birthday I didn't celebrate. This time, I couldn't change my mind, I took the measure of the thing."

When we read her words again, we see that she did not try to have a child at 40 either. Many women have children after this age, and this without any external intervention, without any reproductive help. Others, more numerous, choose to

Psychological reasons for not wanting a child

be helped; in any case, in both cases, it is not impossible to have children. Françoise, for her part, talks about her 40th birthday as a deadline, a limit beyond which she can no longer do anything: "40 was a barrier for me."

Her only fear is to regret it one day. Unlike other women for whom regret is part of the present, Françoise does not doubt for today, but for tomorrow. It is nevertheless very likely that she will never regret it, her lifestyle and her husband rather comforting her in her decision.

"At 40, I felt lost, destabilized. I had my back to the wall. I thought I was the only one in that situation, I didn't dare talk about it, and even today, I don't like talking about it. It's a difficult subject, I find it very hard to talk about it in public, to feel at ease when I'm questioned. I find people very rude, very voyeuristic. As soon as they know that I don't have a child, they say "Oh, you don't have a child?" without any consideration, immediately expecting me to justify myself, to explain such incongruity. I can't stand it! This is part of my private life. Do we ask all parents why they had children? Are they required to justify themselves, to state their motives? Fortunately, the only time I flinched a little was when I was in my 40s. My husband and I talked about it and he made a list of all the things that get in the way of parenting. I agreed with him 100%. I agree with him that when you have a child, you're in for twenty years. After you raise them, you still have to help them find a job, settle down, get married. You have to spend your life saving in case of personal bankruptcy. Alain didn't take me for a ride, he had told me the color before we got married. I knew where I stood. Perhaps, if I had sincerely wanted to become a mother, if it had been vital for me, we would have reconsidered the question, but it never happened. Then I realized that it was a choice that I could make like anyone else, and live well having made it. I never missed a child, I don't see a place for him in the life I had and still have today. At the time, we had sold our first second home and bought a second one, just as dilapidated. We had started very heavy work that required our full involvement. With a child, we would have had to make a clean sweep of it, reorganize our lives from top to bottom, which seemed impossible to me."

Later, in the discussion, Françoise admits that she sometimes felt a little lonely when her husband, then a sales representative, was away.

"I wanted a small dog, so I bought a 2-month-old poodle. He was the joy of my life for seventeen years, I walked him everywhere. I'm not making a comparison with a child, but it shows that I wasn't made to be a mother. You don't have a child just to be lonely. Women who have children for themselves are the real selfish ones.

Chapter 6

Demography and society: is it reasonable to have children today?

Neo-Malthusians

"Our planet is overpopulated," Joshua tells me. "I'm an environmental engineer by training, and I'm quite aware of environmental issues. I am pessimistic about the future of the planet. It doesn't make me want to share that with other humans. As a general rule, I think people should have fewer children, mostly on poor continents, in the third world."

In the wake of the nineteenth-century economic thinker Reverend Thomas Malthus, more and more specialists and non-specialists alike are convinced that overpopulation will lead the planet into an ecological dead end. This catastrophe is, according to them, not only environmental, but also has to do with the survival of the whole Earth. Some of them do not even have a real ecological sensitivity, they fear above all for the conservation of the human species. In France, Yves Cochet and Cousteau in his time, James Lovelock in England, Lester Brown in the United States, belong to this movement.

Isabelle, a doctor in the South of France, is a Cartesian and a historian: "Before, there were wars and a high infant mortality rate, all causes that naturally regulated the population. Today, medicine is constantly pushing the limits at both ends of the life chain. As a result, we have become so numerous that there is no more free space, the cities are over-populated, we are facing a perpetual housing crisis."

Listening to her, I get the impression that she almost regrets the progress made by medicine, in favor of a return to Darwin's law. A surprising cynicism from a disciple of Hippocrates?

From his outpost in Latin America, Hervé has an even deeper and more sensitive vision of the deterioration of the planet and the link between over-birth and ecological disaster. If he spoke to me at length about his first reason for not wanting children, a consequence of his lifestyle and his visceral independence, this mountain guide and inveterate backpacker also puts his finger on another reason, the environmental problems, which reinforces his initial position.

"The Earth is going bad. As a guide, I have access to spectacular places, but for our children (if I had any) or for future generations in general, it will be over. The Galapagos Islands are disappearing, for example. With overpopulation,

No Children. It Makes Sense!

everything has become very complicated. The majority of the world's population lives on 100 dollars a month. All the conflicts over water and poverty will only get worse. These conflicts, they bother me. I don't think it's a gift to be 30 years old in 2040. I feel like everything is accelerating."

The denatality can appear as *the* solution to solve the environmental problems in general, the multiplication of the quantity of waste and greenhouse gases in particular. Fewer children means a less populated planet and therefore less waste production. Presented in this way, the equation does indeed seem logical! The Belgian writer Théophile de Giraud, organizer of the non-parents' festival, highlights in the chapter "Overpollupopulation" of his book *L'Art de guillotiner les procréateurs, an anti-natalist manifesto*, the link that exists between an excess of population and the pollution of the planet.

"We have no chance of saving it, as a livable space for all, by continuing to multiply. Even then, Captain Cousteau estimated that the optimum number of people on Earth would be 800 million. The Third World is in full demographic growth. But it is not up to them to take this problem in hand, as they do not have the material and conceptual means to choose to have few children. It is the West that must set an example by a form of degrowth [...][47]."

"Our planet is crumbling under the weight of the proliferating human species: the most effective way to drastically

---

47. *Terra Eco*, n° 7, October 2009, p. 55.

Demography and society: is it reasonable to have children today?

reduce our ecological footprint is not to give birth to a new consumer-polluter," he writes on his blog.

To understand the ins and outs that motivate neo-Malthusians and anti-natalists, let's first try to put together some numbers and facts.

Demographers predict that we could reach 9 billion inhabitants by 2050! However, this threshold is not confirmed by all specialists[48]. In any case, we are still in a period of population growth and 85% of the energy we use to feed, drive, work, cook and light ourselves is of fossil origin, namely coal, oil and natural gas, which are non-renewable. According to the International Energy Agency (IEA), we would need to increase global energy production by more than 50% by 2030, and almost double electricity production, which are currently mainly fueled by these three energies that have remained the cheapest so far, but also the most polluting. Under these conditions, the IEA predicts a doubling of greenhouse gas emissions in less than a generation.

What can be done to preserve the planet from CO_2 emissions and reduce greenhouse gas emissions? Reducing the number of cars per capita, televisions, cell phones, developing renewable energies, investing in nuclear power, photosynthesis, tidal energy, hydroelectricity, geothermal energy, all this can be the result of governmental measures. To have or not to have children, on the other hand, depends on a

---

48. Read the debate between demographer Henri Leridon and French Green MP Yves Cochet in the monthly *Terra Eco*, n° 7, October 2009.

personal decision, on individual will. Unless we cut off all the state subsidies, which since the Second World War have encouraged population growth through birth control policies.

Anti-natalists thus vilify the idea of a society that promotes children as a source of wealth, which responds to two types of reasoning. The first is consistent with a vision of affluence: to show that "we have the means" to feed, house and raise them. The second reflex, among the most deprived this time, is to consider children as a source of additional manpower: more mouths to feed of course, but also free labor, especially for peasants.

Roland Jaccard, our nihilist philosopher, is ready to make an exception to his antinatalism by joining this last reasoning:

"I can understand a very pragmatic argument in rural societies, where children are made because, after having supported them, they will support their parents. There is also a need for a workforce to work in the fields. In our service societies, this thesis no longer holds."

In the Malthusian idea, having children and being unable to control births are the lot of poor countries. The rich, on the other hand, would be experienced in the art of planning, of controlling the demographic flow. In fact, only authoritarian states have drastically imposed such measures to prevent their populations from having children. The only country to have managed to control its birth rate with convincing results is the People's Republic of China: the famous one-child policy launched in 1978. At the price of what sacrifices and what methods? Forced sterilization campaigns, abortions by

Demography and society: is it reasonable to have children today?

the thousands, especially when Chinese women are pregnant with girls, since only boys guarantee a patrimonial transmission (the ratio is 124 male babies for 100 female babies). China, with 1.338 billion inhabitants, has almost succeeded in stabilizing its population growth. India, the most populous country in the world after China, is often cited as one of the states that have used one-child policies, but the campaigns have failed. The mentality is not compatible with the massive use of contraception. India's fertility rate is 2.7 children per woman, compared to 1.7 in China. As a result, the Indian population is expected to reach 1.5 billion by 2050.

In Latin America, it's even worse. Hervé makes me observe the situation:

"Here, fertility rates are around 3 and 4. Peru cannot feed all its inhabitants (68% of the urban population lives in slums). I don't like the repressive system, but people should be made to understand not to have so many children."

Without being a supporter of totalitarianism, he admits that the situation has become so critical that it is absolutely necessary for governments to get involved. The birth rate is no longer a strictly private matter. Thus, he is frightened when he hears the official discourse held by the so-called "modern" Western countries.

"The position of Western governments, especially France, is becoming untenable, even if the problem is less than in Latin America or Africa: we cannot continue to tell people to have even more children to pay for their pensions. The reality is that there is not enough work for everyone.

The green deputy Yves Cochet, former Minister of Regional Planning and the Environment, is just as radical:

"I have spent 99% of my time for the past 35 years fighting for behavioural change. I'm very sad about that, but I realize that things are not moving fast enough. So I say we have to play on the demographic variable as well if we want to have any chance of success[49]."

According to a British non-governmental organization, the *Optimum Population Trust*[50], condoms are the solution to all our problems, not just a bulwark against sexually transmitted diseases. In an article published in September 2009, the think tank shows that, in order to reduce greenhouse gas emissions, it would be 4 to 5 times more effective to invest in the promotion of contraception (through family planning among others) rather than in low-carbon technologies. It is much cheaper to reduce births than to invest on a large scale in solar panels or wind turbines! The NGO relied on a report prepared by the *London School of Economics*. Investing in contraception would cost society around $7, compared to $24 for an investment in wind power, $51 in solar power and $83 in carbon dioxide reduction. The OPT study estimates that by investing $220 billion over the next 40 years, it would be possible to prevent half of all births and thus reduce the volume of CO2 by 34 billion tons. Another study, conducted by the University of Oregon, puts the United States in the dock. Each American baby would be responsible for the

49. *In Terra Eco*, October 2009.
50. http://www.optimumpopulation.org/

emission of 1,644 tons of CO2, i.e. 5 times more than a Chinese baby and 91 times more than a Bangladeshi child. An aggravating factor is the high life expectancy.

Discussing overpopulation in these terms quickly becomes dangerous and tricky. These questions raised by demographers, economists and politicians sometimes take a strange turn for the worse. What to think of Pascal Riché when he writes in *Libération*[51] "Malthus was right, hell is the baby. It kills development"? His article made waves, sometimes interpreted as a vindication with fascist overtones. For some, the anti-populationist credo aims to disguise the genocide of peoples, for others, it is a salutary alarm bell. Let's just remember that the food crisis in the world kills 24,000 people a day, including 16,000 children.

From an ethical point of view, intervening on the number of births to reduce them is a contested approach. The Catholic Church is fiercely opposed to it. Yves Cochet points out in an article in the magazine *Terra Eco*[52] that these questions "touch on the most intimate aspects. In the eyes of the Church, birth control is still taboo. Pope Benedict XVI, and John Paul II before him, is firmly opposed to abortion. The use of condoms is more complicated: officially, the

---

51. RICHÉ (Pascal), "Malthus was right, hell is the baby. It kills development," *Libération*, April 30, 1992.
52. "The birth of one European is equivalent, in terms of impact, to that of ten Congolese", debate between Yves Cochet and Henri Leridon, *Terra Eco*, n° 7, October 2009, p. 46.

No Children. It Makes Sense!

doctrine forbids it; unofficially, many priests tolerate it, advise it, and sometimes, on rare occasions, distribute them. In any case, procreation is an essential, central fact of Christianity. The Church's social doctrine is essentially concerned with families. According to the Christian writer and demographer René Valette, this is what is called "doctrinal natalism". Meeting in Zagreb in October 2010, the European bishops deplored the "demographic winter" that has befallen Europe and encouraged states to promote the birth rate through support for families and a change in culture.

Single people and "childless" couples are still far from their concerns...

The pessimists

The more the Earth is populated, the more the problems of violence, famine and unemployment are accentuated. Famine in particular is linked to the environment. The link has become so indisputable for a large number of specialists (demographers, geographers, scientists, UN observers) that the so-called "green" political parties have taken up the subject for several years.

"Giving life to a child in the world as it is today and as it will be tomorrow does not feel like a gift. Why not? Look at the conflicts, they never stop, they happen on almost every continent at regular intervals," Joshua points out to me.

Demography and society: is it reasonable to have children today?

To have children while the world drags behind it a cohort of threats? "No thank you", all the catastrophists, the tormented, the anxious, the pessimists, the worried and the rationalists answer in chorus.

"Perhaps you have chosen not to reproduce for the love of the child you will never have: it is true that it is less and less good to be born in our Darwinian society and that nothingness remains the best citadel against the assaults of fate or the ravages of inflation. Your non-progeny will not end up unemployed or in the public social action center; nor will it risk leading a sad life as a wage earner while waiting to die of cancer, or worse, of old age. She thanks you from the depths of her soft night cocoon[53]. In the voice of this Cassandra, you will not be surprised to recognize Théophile de Giraud once again.

Without knowing each other, he and Joshua are perfectly on the same wavelength:

"We live in an increasingly precarious world, which is absolutely not comparable to that of our parents. Is it reasonable to have children? The problem is severalfold: if I became a father one day, would I be physically fit enough? Health concerns can seriously jeopardize the situation. Mentally, would I be open enough, financially, solvent enough? Unemployment and professional insecurity are undermining the prospects of an easy end to a career. Everything has become too uncertain and difficult these days.

---

53. http://nonparents.skynetblogs.be/archive/2010/02/24/pour-celebrer-les-childfree.html

Isabelle reverses the equation. For her, it's simple, "you can only have children out of recklessness or in a spirit of euphoria. Children are reserved for optimists."

"Some people may think I'm a pessimist, but I think I'm a realist! I had a brother, he committed suicide at the age of 23, I was 28. When I think back to my mother: she suffered so much, if she had known in advance all that my brother would do to her, would she have wanted it so much? The *fatum* is frightening! To take this risk seemed to me unspeakable, unthinkable. One day, she concludes, a child fell asleep against me, I could not move, I realized the fragility of such a being. It starts with the meeting of two cells and ends with a being of flesh and blood. I don't leave much room for the ideal, I prevent myself from dreaming, because I know too well the harmful consequences. Even maternal love is selfish, it is an exchange too often based on the 'give and take'. I believe very little in the sublime."

Why not adopt?

Every year, French children are placed in homes as a result of births under X, abandonment, the death of their parents or abuse. There are approximately 3,000 wards of the State (not to be confused with wards of the Nation, who are war orphans), which is a small number compared to the total number of children placed in foster care: 23,000 (figures given by the Ministry of Foreign Affairs for 2006).

Before being declared judicially abandoned, a child remains in care for an average of six years. Of the 3,000 "adoptable" children, one third have health problems, disabilities, live with siblings or are over 2 years old. All these criteria explain, among other things, why families applying for adoption turn to foreign countries (eight times out of ten). But beware, adoption abroad remains expensive: between 10,000 and 20,000 euros! The process is often long, tedious and administrative[54].

Since 2005, international adoptions in France have decreased by 24%. For 8,000 approvals granted each year by the General Councils, 4,000 children were adopted in 2006 compared to 3,062 in 2007. Among the most important countries are Ethiopia (417 in 2007), Haiti (403) and Russia (402), followed by Colombia (375) and Vietnam (268). Brazil and China are no longer among the countries of choice. There are many reasons why France lags behind countries such as Italy, Spain and the United States. First, the selection criteria: in France, only 23% of adopted children are over 5 years old. In Italy, this figure exceeds 50%. Second, our neighbors have

---

54. The French adoption agency was inaugurated in 2006. It is an organization under the supervision of the State, of which the General Councils are members and partners. It is also a legal entity with a legal status of intermediary for adoption. Its main mission is to inform and advise families who have received approval and to facilitate and secure their procedures abroad. http://www. agence-adoption.fr/ Alongside it, there are forty-two Authorized Adoption Agencies (AAA), under private law, authorized for international adoption. They help in the preparation of the project, and provide information on the technical and legal aspects of the procedure.

a very proactive humanitarian policy (significant funding and actions promoted through diplomatic channels). Finally, the presence of nuns (Italian and Spanish in particular) in the orphanages of the countries of origin favors the attribution of children to their compatriots.

At first, I thought that a person who doesn't want to have children would also be reluctant to adopt them. I was wrong: "having" children does not necessarily mean "biological bonding". Take, for example, women who do not want to be pregnant[55]. To have a child without going through the maternity box? Eureka, they have the solution: adoption. Forget the pain of pregnancy and childbirth. After an obstacle course that can last several years, they have a baby or a child in their arms that they will have to raise and love as their own. The difference with the biological parents tends to disappear. These women are no longer considered as childless women, but as mothers in their own right.

To those who raise as a main argument to protect the planet against overpopulation, adoption also seems to be a ready-made answer. We can indeed consider that by adopting, we save a child who is already present on Earth anyway. A child who did not ask to come into the world, who often arrived in very difficult conditions, whether economic, social or psychological. In spite of these good feelings and sharpened reasonings, some people continue to be opposed

---

55. See Chapter 4.

Demography and society: is it reasonable to have children today?

to it while others value this approach. Why and what are their arguments against?

"I'm very divided," Joshua explains. "I don't believe in it very much, because it's still an uprooting, the child loses his original culture."

Isabelle agrees even more categorically:

"I think adoption is even worse, couples who adopt are hit even harder than others, because children are taken away from their natural environment, their culture, their country even sometimes. It's acculturation."

Cedric joins them:

"Adopting, in my eyes, is almost worse; it's once again wanting to appear generous, to have a perfect little family to show off. To me, having children at all costs is a proof of vanity, it is believing oneself to be eternal or wanting to be like that."

Beside these extreme points of view, Marie and Anne ask themselves or have asked themselves the question: "Adoption? Maybe in ten years, why not?" As for the second, she says she "never considered adoption as a realistic option, because my relationship was not strong enough. Then I didn't think about it anymore."

Roland Jaccard, however, sums up the opinion shared by most people I have interviewed on the issue:

"Adoption is great for people who want to have children and can't physically or can't manage to have children."

In the end, the majority of "childless" people are against adoption, not systematically out of dogmatism or principle, but because their lack of desire for maternity or paternity is also a lack of desire for parenthood. Whether or not it is genetically theirs, a child remains a child to be cared for all his life. All the burdens mentioned in the previous chapters fall equally on the biological or adoptive parents.

Chapter 7

Is the child too expensive?

A minority argument not to be taken lightly

The financial argument is not at all significant among those put forward by the "childless"; on the contrary, we note that in the socially disadvantaged classes, the number of women without children (married or not), unemployed, not having a good level of education, is less important than in the rest of the population. The financial issue is only raised by some (mostly men), but never as a driving, decisive factor. Nevertheless, it should not be underestimated or eradicated.

Let's remember Jennifer who has been in a relationship for seven and a half years with Johann, nine years younger than her.

"I would certainly have an easier time conceiving of a family life if I had the means. Indeed, I saw my grandparents deprive themselves hard for me. I always told myself that

I would never go without for a kid who would spit in my face in ten years! I don't want to turn into *Wonder Woman* either: taking on a job as a senior executive to earn a higher salary than I currently do, being able to put up with staggered or very long hours, and having to hire a nanny to watch my kids at home for me, is not my thing! If I had one or more children, I would love to raise them myself. But I'm not willing to pay the price financially."

Suzanne, a legal secretary and single woman, sees it too:

"Looking back, I'm really glad I didn't have a child. I see how it is with other women, I think you have to have a lot of income to raise them. You only have one life! Mine is pleasant: I am very independent and I am happy like that. I don't suffer from it. I have often worked in international firms, I like my job. I have also worked for big names in ready-to-wear. Paris is a fascinating city, there is always an exhibition to discover, friends to see. I also travel often, I have no ties, which allows me to change jobs and life as I please. I even lived six months in the United States. I live intensely. If I am not rich financially, I am rich culturally."

Victor, younger than most of the people I interviewed, belongs to this "precarious" generation particularly affected by unemployment, poorly paid or without money to support himself. At 29 years old, he is a nomad who has traveled a lot and is currently in England where he works as a volunteer in a community center that offers leisure activities for young people in difficulty, from disadvantaged classes, or with disabilities.

"For me, it's a challenge. I work with children from 6 to 18 years old. I had already been an animator in France on a work camp project, the organization of a medieval festival in Auvergne. This time, it's a different setting. I am never alone with the children, I am still in the observation phase. We lead games and sports sessions in schools, with hoops, balls, we also offer soccer and basketball sessions. It's a sport-based training. At the same time, we work on sexual problems, drugs, violence, and daily life. Some of the children have mild disabilities. Sport is a means of integration, an instrument of social cohesion too. I am a rather open and sociable person, I like to talk to people, with this job, I try to understand what young people have in their head. I don't always succeed!"

When I listen to him, I think that his experience is quite exceptional for a boy of his age. I am looking at someone who learns every day how to deal with teenagers and children, who are also damaged by life. Wouldn't he want to be one of them later on?

"Thinking of having children myself? I am not financially comfortable enough: I go from one fixed-term contract to another. At the moment, I only earn the equivalent of a salary and in exchange I am provided with accommodation. It is not much, so I have to work on the side to complete my income, to buy clothes or a train ticket when I want to go back to France. For the moment, my income has been rather minimal, enough to live, to find a place to stay and barely enough to get dressed. I don't have room for anything

Is the child too expensive?

superfluous or to support a family. I have a 32 year old sister with a 6 month old baby and she confirms that there are impossible choices with a child."

Joshua, on the other hand, while earning a good living, is very attached to his financial freedom:

"The older you get, the more you get used to a certain quality of life, to your own little comfort, and I would find it very hard to go back to that, to give up those tiny pleasures. To give up this life for a child? I am not ready. Will I ever be? I don't think so."

The reflections of some and others are cries of the heart, but all this remains random and vague. Mathematically, is it possible to put a figure on this cost?

In July 1994, Simone Veil, then Minister of Social Affairs, proposed a law (which was passed as the "Family Law"). Article 40 stipulated that "the High Council for Population and Family Affairs would draw up an annual report evaluating the cost of children", specifying that this report should be the result of collaboration between the National Union of Family Associations, INSEE and INED. As soon as it was published in the *Official Journal*, the idea was surreptitiously buried. Why was this? Was it wishful thinking or an unachievable task? Is it because, as Joël-Yves Le Bigot, president of the "Institut de l'enfant", said, "all those who are concerned about the country's demographics say that it is better that the French do not really know how much it costs to raise children, otherwise they would have even fewer children[56]"?

When calculating a budget dedicated to the child, how can we distinguish between the expenses that are directly attributable to the child?

We should already agree on the definition of the cost of a child. In 1989, INSEE developed a method of calculation; the cost would correspond to the additional sum needed by a household when it welcomes a child to enjoy the same standard of living as before. If you have a child with the same income - even if that income is high - your standard of living is bound to go down, since there are now three people on that budget. How much would it have to be increased for the couple to continue to enjoy the same standard of living as before?

Based on this method of calculation, INSEE concluded that a family's child budget amounted to 20 percent of income. At the time, the median French salary was 20,500 francs (3,125 euros), so it was stated that a child cost an average of 4,100 francs (625 euros) per month, so 49,200 francs (7,500 euros) per year, nearly 900,000 francs (137,200 euros) to support him or her until they reached majority. Experts on all sides were up in arms: "Much too high, even absolutely

56. *Le Point*, article published on September 5, 1998. http://www.lepoint.fr/archives/article.php/77384Conference given by Joël-Yves Le Bigot organized by the Direction générale de la concurrence, de la consommation et de la répression des fraudes, March 23, 2000, http://www.minefi.gouv.fr/fonds_documentaire/dgccrf/02_actualite/ateliers_conso/atelier14.htmFrom the same author: *Vive les 11-25*, Editions Eyrolles; *Au secours, j'embauche un jeune*, Editions Dunod.

exaggerated, in any case totally unrealistic", according to economists; "a little high", according to the public authorities; "fair enough" for family associations... No one agreed. So how do we know?

In fact, as is often the case, it is all a matter of nuance: the effort made by a couple earning twice the minimum wage compared to a couple earning three or four times the minimum wage is not comparable. Even if in the case of the second couple, there is also a loss of purchasing power, it is less serious and less noticeable, because it does not jeopardize vital needs (food, housing, clothing). Secondly, a baby, a child or a teenager do not generate the same expenses. "A child under the age of 14 weighs about half as much as an adult or teenager in consumption," write Jean-Michel Hourriez and Lucile Olier, the authors of a study published in *Économie et statistique*[57]. From birth to age 4, the budget is heavily burdened by equipment expenses (baby carriage, stroller, bed, wardrobe, changing table, etc.). After the age of 4, the budget is reduced. On the other hand, starting secondary school is a painful threshold to cross. The cost of a child from 11 to 15 years old, who is entering adolescence, then increases sharply (he wants his own room, is crying out for pocket money, becomes a *fashion victim*, starts going to the movies, needs more expensive sports equipment, etc.). From 15 to 18 years old, his cost is equivalent to that of an

---

57. *In* Hourriez (Jean-Michel) and Olier (Lucile), "Niveau de vie et taille du ménage : estimations d'une échelle d'équivalence", *Économie et statistique*, n°308-309-310, published by Insee, October 1997.

No Children. It Makes Sense!

adult. Think you're done? No way! The "adulescent", which many of us have been ourselves, will be happy to remain clinging to his room and your living room. How to put out the flesh of his flesh? It is not uncommon to see young adults extend their parental stay until they are 25 or 28 years old, even after they get their first job.

Finally, the cost isn't always the same. What about the time spent by new mothers? Is it part of the budget? How do you value it? If a mother decides to cook her child's meals instead of buying ready-made food, if she knits her child woollen cardigans and sews her little dresses instead of going to the store to buy them, how can we evaluate the hourly cost of these activities? Economists speak of an "opportunity cost", i.e. the money that parents could have earned by working, if they had not had to go home to look after their child. Behind this expression, we can add maternity leave, days spent at the bedside of a sick child, hours spent at the end of school, school meetings, Wednesday afternoons dedicated to activities, school outings, etc., all of which prevent them from working overtime, obtaining a promotion, taking professional training and therefore receiving raises in the long run.

It's true that at this rate, these are sobering arguments!

And yet...

Is the child too expensive?

Aid and natalist policies

In France, the fiscal and social leverage is more likely to tip the balance in favor of the natalists. There is indeed an arsenal of public aid (family allowances, share of the child in the tax household, SNCF and RATP discount cards) and private aid (airline companies, low-cost sports activities, etc.). A whole set of measures that is itself decried and denounced by anti-natalists and neo-Malthusians. The latter would, on the contrary, like the State to be neutral on this point and no longer get involved in fertility (for example, as in the United States).

However, the family lobbies are not satisfied either; in their eyes, these aids are not adapted: in France, a couple who has its first child does not receive aids from the family allowances (unless they have extremely low incomes), and the same goes for the famous birth bonus. On the other hand, the aid becomes significant after the third child. However, the majority of French families will not have any. The fact remains that children cost the State a lot of money: family allowances currently pay 124 euros per month for two children, 283 euros for three and, from the fourth child on, 159 euros per additional child. If we add to this the problem of pensions, the French welfare system is explosive. The elderly, like children, represent an increasingly important cost for society. But, paradoxically, babies are also the future adults who will finance these expenses. In our system, as it is conceived today, the snake is biting its own tail.

No kid convinced, Isabelle, who belongs to the medical profession, questions herself on this dilemma, especially when she notices the progress made by medicine to prolong life at all costs.

"If we do not rejuvenate society and if we live only among pensioners, who will pay for the pensions? A society of old people is a society of condemned people, who will support them? Medicine is adding to it, trying to get eternity, it's playing the sorcerer's apprentice, but I think the pendulum will eventually swing back the other way."

So to have or not to have children? What is the most economically viable solution? The question of who will add to the Social Security deficit in the future is far from over.

Chapter 8

When philosophical convictions take precedence

Religious commitment: the gift of faith

I met Paul exactly four days before his retirement from the world... Paul is going to become a monk. As I write this, he is now living in an abbey and devoting himself to prayer. It's hard to imagine when I see him arrive at our appointment, dressed like any modern man, with a motorcycle helmet on his arm.

By putting himself at the service of God, through prayer and by following the Rule (regular order, he crossed out the possibility of marrying and having a family). How does one live the abandonment of having one's own children? Is this choice similar to that of other lay men who wish not to be fathers?

"I have four brothers: one older and three younger. I was raised in a religious and churchgoing family, however, I would not describe my personal practice as "active". I was a follower of the movement, even though I always felt like I believed in God. My first call was when I was 12 years old. I was at mass and looking at the priest, I said to myself: why not me? At 18, I had a second call and then a third at 24. This time it was more serious. I was on a very important pilgrimage to Bosnia-Herzegovina. There, I really had a personal encounter with God, it was in a parish during the adoration of a holy sacrament. It is said that there were apparitions of the Blessed Virgin in that place. From that moment on, I became a volunteer; I was no longer a passive believer, I took it upon myself to go to Mass regularly, I was determined to be an actor of my faith. Until the day I decided to enter the seminary. I was 29 years old."

Ten years later, he was on his way to becoming a Trappist monk. The origin of the word monk, *monos* in Greek, means "alone, unique". The monk is alone with God and with his community.

"I am a candidate and the Church needs seven years to confirm me. She can tell you no thanks, it's not for you! The wisdom of the Church, expressed in the Rule of St. Benedict, has decided that it takes a certain number of years to become a real monk. After the first year of postulancy with the monks, I will receive a new name and a novice's habit to practice my novitiate. Three years later, I will make my first temporary vows of profession of faith, and I will wait another three years. Then comes the time of final vows. Unlike priests, in the monastic life there is only one judge and decision-maker, the father-master (who is appointed by the father-abbot). He evaluates everything that is not spiritual (work, community life, etc.). We have meetings once a week with him."

Listening to him, I wonder about the vows taken by monks and priests: are they the same?

"The parish priests, diocesan priests and bishops of the secular clergy live in the Century, that is, in the world in the midst of the laity, dedicating themselves to preaching. They do not take vows of poverty, chastity or obedience, but commit themselves to celibacy and to obey their bishop. A parish priest, a bishop and some monks are also priests, just as there are priests without a parish, such as vicars who are dependent on a diocese (secular priests), and others who are dependent on a monastic order (regular priests eligible as abbots). Monks and regular priests take a vow of poverty, chastity and obedience."

If I play on words, I would say that "single" today does not mean "childless" and that the two concepts are not incompatible. Many men are fathers without being bound either by marriage or by any contract (PACS, for example). Paul replies that "celibate" is understood in the medieval sense of the term (11th century): without a concubine and without children. There are several reasons for this rule. First of all, priests want to live as Christ lived on earth, and Jesus was not married and had no children. Secondly, the

When philosophical convictions take precedence

priest could not support a family. Today, a priest is housed and earns about 800 euros per month.

"In my religion, the Roman Catholic discipline, only celibate men are called to the priesthood. Therefore, none of them can logically have children. On the other hand, this rule does not apply among Eastern Catholics: there can be married priests, because they follow another rite, although they also depend on the pope. Among the Orthodox, some depend on the Patriarchate, others on Constantinople. Among the Protestants also, pastors can be married."

Far be it from me to judge him and to challenge the rule of celibacy among Catholics. That is not the object of the debate nor of my investigation. On the other hand, I would like to know how he, as an individual, as a man, manages and feels about this renunciation. Does he consider it a sacrifice?

"I've always dreamed of getting married," he says. "My older brother has four kids, they're adorable, and of course when I see them, I totally fall for them. To have children in my turn? Yes, surely, in the absolute, I would have liked, but I already don't like this verb 'to have'. I also hate the expression 'to have the right' for a child. A couple does not have a right to a child, they receive a child. However, each one has its vocation, its life project. I was touched by what is called grace, which makes it possible to bear this ordeal. I did not choose it. I understand why I will not have children, why I cannot get married and I accept it. I agree with the rabbis, for example, they are right to say that it is not natural. There is a super-natural dimension to this commitment. I think I will have different satisfactions in the exercise of my faith. I will have other experiences of fatherhood because of it. I feel that I have a concrete faith, I don't think I am a mystic. I live the word of God, I try to understand what it means today. Over the years, I have realized that my character is more suited to prayer and community life. [...] Finally, I would like to conclude with a question that is on the minds of many Christians (and non-Christians), because I think it is related to your topic. I am often asked why women cannot be ordained as priests. It is not an inequality between the two sexes, it is a matter of the ontology of the person. In each being, there is a particular call to live as a woman or as a man. Thus, women can give life while men cannot. The priest will not be a father, will not have children, but he gives life in another way, during the Eucharist. Through his hands, the bread becomes the body of Christ, and the wine the blood of Christ. He gives life to the faithful. This is another form of fruitfulness."

On a subject as feminine as motherhood, I obviously needed a woman's testimony. It was out of the question for me to be satisfied with a priest or a monk to approach parenthood and the place of the child among religious. I was very lucky to be able to meet Soizic, alias Sister Marie-Thérèse, a religious in a congregation of apostolic life in the Paris region.

Sister Marie-Thérèse is 63 years old and she entered the orders at the age of 22, first as an observation (at the postulancy) and then definitively, three years later. This testimony is even dearer to me than the previous one, because it is very

When philosophical convictions take precedence

rare to be able to hear the words of a religious on such a sensitive subject - the renunciation of motherhood, sexual relations, tenderness with a man and the question of the couple are not taboo subjects, but they are discreet, complicated and difficult to approach. Soizic is old enough to be a grandmother and she was doubly open-minded. She spoke to me extremely freely, with fabulous kindness and insight. To be honest, I was first afraid of disturbing her, then I was afraid that the interview would be "politically correct" and too brief. In the end, Sister Marie-Thérèse surprised me with her simplicity and vivacity. Apparently, she was very interested in my subject, she asked me questions, and our meeting resembled more a real exchange, a casual conversation, than a classic interview.

Soizic comes from a rural background, her parents are farmers, "we were neither rich nor poor". She has three brothers, an older one and two younger ones.

"We are quite close in age, so we were raised together, I have good childhood memories, we all played with dolls. However, pretty soon, the tasks at home were not divided equally between the boys and the only girl in the couple. We went to boarding school in middle school and when we came home on weekends, I did the housework with my mother, while my brothers were assigned to work outside, with the animals and in the fields. The division of labor took care of itself. I went to university, in Besançon, I had male friends, at the university of course, but also in adolescence, my brothers' friends. I was in the Faculty of Letters with a major in philosophy: I quickly got bored, I was disappointed, it seemed empty to me. The theme of the first year was death and I wanted to work on life, I had in mind for a long time to have a job to help others. I wanted to be an educator. At the end of the second year, I went to North Africa, to an orphanage run by nuns. This experience was disappointing, I came up against the management of the sisters, but it didn't take me away from my vocation at all. It was there that I really made the decision to enter the orders.

At the time, the French education system was desperately short of teachers. Although Soizic had not yet finished her studies, she was nevertheless offered a position as a French and English teacher in a sixth grade class. She accepted, somewhat reluctantly. When she returned to France in 1968, she worked for another year.

"My brothers were in college in Besançon, they were among the students who participated in the demonstrations. At the end of that year, I expressed my desire to become a sister, but I did not want to be a contemplative. I wanted to be at the service of others, to be in contact with society. One of my cousins who was a social worker told me about the Congregation that would become mine. It is directed exclusively towards the disadvantaged social classes. It is present in several cities in France and spread throughout the world. Some of the sisters live in the heart of the cities, among the people they want to help; this attracted me very much."

The Congregation requires a three-year preparation. Soizic must also take vows of obedience, chastity and poverty.

When philosophical convictions take precedence

Is it easy to resolve, at 22 years old, to no longer experience carnal contact? Did she easily mourn the loss of children and motherhood? Soizic does not try to escape my questions. With her soft voice, she answers me that the most difficult thing was to succeed in doing without a man, to live in solitude and abstinence. The first year of training was the year of "the struggle":

"It was not possible, unimaginable. I was destined to be a nun, but I was still a woman like any other. This perspective, this third point, the vow of chastity, seemed to me from the start to be the most problematic to pronounce. I'm not just talking about sexual relations. A woman also needs tenderness. The prospect of no longer being able to snuggle up to a man frightened me, so much so that at first I thought I couldn't do it!"

Soizic is going through ups and downs and is especially going through a big period of doubt.

"I had terrible crises, I cried a lot, I couldn't make a decision. I thought it was a mountain to leave men, marriage, and life as a couple behind."

Her supervisor, Sister Superior, granted her a leave of absence during the Christmas vacations to return to her family and reflect. Perhaps this extreme form of commitment was not for her.

"I thought about it, I thought about the proposals that men had made to me. At least twice I was told that if I wanted to get married, the door was wide open. I knew one man in particular in North Africa to whom I could have said yes. But

I never experienced what is called love at first sight. Perhaps I was too idealistic? I expected more than that. I wanted certainty, I wanted to be totally excited. By comparison, when I was considering my life in the Congregation, everything seemed extraordinary. If I had married, I would have wanted to live among the poor anyway, to give to others, to be involved in education. I don't think that the men who courted me understood this desire. It was not a whim that would pass me by. But what they were offering me was a traditional bourgeois life."

Has she ever been in love, has she ever felt her heart beat for boys? Soizic remains cryptic when she talks about her suitors. By modesty or desire not to say too much. She continues her story.

"When I returned after the Christmas vacations, my faith had not left me. I felt like I had found my way. I went on a retreat in the spring and heard a voice saying, 'Let me live in you.' Suddenly, I resolved my inner conflict and went to my superior and told her I was staying."

Soizic joined a small religious community: "It was fantastic, I had my place." However, eleven years later, she had a breakdown. "I had not been attentive to the signs that should have alerted me. I had given up on sexuality, but I had not sufficiently considered the lack of tenderness and my real need. Still, I didn't want to give up. So I went into psychotherapy with a psychoanalyst who did not specifically treat religious people." Soizic came out of it stronger, with a better understanding of her trajectory, her choices, and more easily

When philosophical convictions take precedence

accepted the concessions and shortcomings imposed by her vocation. What was her family's reaction to her decision?

"My parents did not understand, especially after my bad experience in North Africa. It's true that I had come back from the orphanage criticizing what I had seen there, the attitude of the sisters, I didn't get along with them."

In the parental mentality, a woman must marry and have children. If not, they feel like failures. They didn't understand how their daughter could thrive in isolation.

"It didn't cost me to not have children and to not know motherhood. When I was young, I had a good time with them by being at the service of families, I simply took care of the little ones. I preferred the company of mothers to children; I did my job with them without any particular qualms. And then my nieces were 5, 6, 7 years old and the dialogue with them touched me... I liked this age of questioning, the discovery of the world with them; even if I saw them little, they really counted for me and I thought that having children was really beautiful. But that was all. And then one day I was old enough to be a grandmother and in my work I discovered the exciting relationship with children... I went to them more easily. That is to say, at that time, this relationship interested and touched me more than ever. I enjoyed their company, observing them playing or dreaming... Contemplating the freshness of their emerging life, their energy, their taste for life, welcoming their tenderness, their look, their smile or laughter, their outstretched hand... everything became a real joy for me in the bond I had with them. This did not make me regret not having had a child myself. Children exist, that is good, even very good. A friend once told me that I had had many children, yes, but not 24 hours a day. On the other hand, I believe that a life is fruitful beyond the children that one has or not. Relationships with others can be relationships where we give ourselves life. This is open to anyone, whether they are a mother or not. The trust we place in each other is a source of life and this is given to all. I remember a wonderful little boy, a little one with red hair, blue eyes, an intuitive heart and luscious words; he runs to his mom one day saying, 'Mom, Mom, Soizic she trusts me!" I had told him that he could trust himself, he knew how to wipe the dishes, he didn't have to keep asking me if it was okay. Another day, he said to me while eating his lunch, "Did you do it? - No, I didn't do it, your mom did. He insists: - No, it's you... - No, it's your mom... Why are you telling me it's me? - It has a little taste of you.' I remain on this marvelous word that lived in me for a long time... and still now."

The nihilists

At first sight, no common point between nihilists and religious people. The conception and the acceptance of a God separate them forever. Their only point of convergence? Not to have children. The first ones because they were called by God and touched by grace, the second ones because they don't believe in anything, denying the necessity to reproduce, partisans of a radical philosophy and dreaming of a "planetary euthanasia".

"To want children is to want revenge for one's past. It is for the woman to give her own mother a gift of her hatred and for the man to compete with his father or with God in the imbecilic fantasy of a posterity. And it is for each couple a remedy to despair. When life has deceived our expectations, when we have given up on creating ourselves, when we feel that everything is ruined, then rather than going to the morgue, we invite our family and loved ones to an even more sinister place, because it is more kitschy: maternity. On the dirty work of humanity, secrecy must reign. Nihilism begins where the will to deceive oneself ceases. But without this will, we would have neither drunkenness, nor art, nor love. So let's make 'as if'... and let the party begin! On its magnificence depend the extent of our wrecks and the brightness of our lucidity. And perhaps we will be strong enough one day to love our midnight as we love the dawn!"

So writes Roland Jaccard in his book *La Tentation nihiliste*[58]. Who are the nihilists? Like the writer, they are often disciples of Schopenhauer and Cioran - as the latter admirably summed up in this sentence, "I aspire to 'have committed all crimes, except that of being a father,'" Roland Jaccard tells me from the outset - and take a certain interpretation of Buddhism (when the cycle of births stops).

---

58. JACCARD (Roland), *La Tentation nihiliste*, Biblio essais, n°4396, Le Livre de Poche, 2006, p. 26.

No Children. It Makes Sense!

"Living has some good sides," concedes Roland Jaccard, "but on the whole, I think I would have preferred not to be born. Maybe we didn't try hard enough not to come into the world at all! This does not mean that my life has been a succession of disasters, hard knocks and dramas."

This conviction came to him very early on:

"Starting in my fifteenth year, I began to think that life was a gigantic mistake. My position on this subject was born from readings and observations. Why consciously inflict this ordeal on a being that does not yet exist and that did not ask to be born? I would prefer not" is the motto of Bartleby, to whom I feel very close. I naively thought that everyone shared my views and quickly realized that this was not the case. Most people don't come to the same conclusion, they are happy to be there. They have no problem with the idea of perpetuating the species. I place myself in the Buddhist tradition, which explains that at some point the cycle of births and rebirths must stop. Besides, who says that one will get along with one's children? Nothing is less certain. I was born in 1941, so I did not suffer directly from the war, which did not prevent me from becoming aware of the atrocities committed during the war. History is a succession of mistreatments inflicted by Man on Man. To have children is in a way to contribute to the perpetuation of the fundamental cruelty of the human condition. The only real success one can dream of is a kind of general suicide. I do not want to add to my personal wreckage the probable drowning of an individual who did not ask for it."

When philosophical convictions take precedence

A position "necessarily in the minority," he admits. However, he is not the only one to think so, he hastens to add.

"My mother also thought it was wrong to bring children into the world. What struck me was that the people who shared my conception were from more privileged classes. I was not abandoned, I was not a beaten child, nobody sexually abused me, my family was loving, on the whole, I had a balanced childhood, in Switzerland on the shores of Lake Geneva [Editor's note: he will tell me, much later in the interview, that his father and grandfather committed suicide], I did not have a specific reason to complain more than any other adolescent. I don't have any siblings, yet I wasn't lonely, I was pretty social with lots of friends."

Roland Jaccard quotes Thomas Bernhard on "the joy of giving birth to children":

"People are mistaken when they think they are giving birth to children. They give birth to an innkeeper or a war criminal, sweating, ugly, with a belly, that's who they give birth to, not children. So people say they are going to have a little baby, but in reality they have an octogenarian who pisses water everywhere, who stinks and is blind and limping and whose gout prevents him from moving, that's the one they give birth to. But that one they don't see, so that nature can perpetuate itself and the same shit goes on forever."

Among the writer's friends are the Swiss psychoanalyst Eric Vartzbed and the South African psychoanalyst David Benatar, author of an "admirable essay": *Better Never to Have*

Been. The Harm of Coming into Existence[59]. If the latter are busy organizing anti-natalist congresses, Roland Jaccard, for his part, "does not profess anything".

"I am not a militant," he says, "except for the non-parents' party, which he attended in May 2009 in Brussels with Théophile de Giraud and Corinne Maier. I am content to obey this feeling, which has always been obvious to me."

The relationship with death

How can we not talk about death when discussing a subject such as whether or not to give life? Although our society tends to hide it, death is omnipresent. Very early sometimes, even before birth - miscarriages are numerous, even if the subject is taboo, because it is extremely badly lived by the parturients, even more in a society where we make less children and where everything is ultra-medicalized - then during the first weeks of life of the infant (sudden death, so much feared by the young parents), and finally throughout the life of the child, the teenager and the adult.

"Philosophically, a child forces us to ask ourselves the question of why", Isabelle rightly tells me.

Few of my participants have spontaneously spoken to me about death, and yet, whether it is a discreet shadow or, on the contrary, indecent and unashamed, it prowls on the horizon

---

59. BENATAR (David), *Better Never to Have Been. The Harm of Coming into Existence*, Oxford University Press, 2006.

When philosophical convictions take precedence

of our destinies, surrounding us and disturbing us. Isabelle analyzes childbirth in the light of posterity. The question for her is to accept or not to have a "zero descent".

"If we don't have children and we die, there is nothing left of us on Earth. Humanity is very confused by this equation. Personally, I'm amazed at the need for everyone to want to continue living. It's quite fascinating, this need to perpetuate the race, to leave a trace. In my opinion, only certain geniuses leave a trace behind them. Not being an exceptional being, I accept not to leave one behind me. The day I disappear, it will not upset anyone.

Another of my speakers, who immediately made the connection between her lack of desire for a child and her conception of death, is a writer. She has placed death at the heart of her novels, perhaps to better tame it. While so many well-known figures (writers, actresses, singers, business leaders) have refused to speak openly about my subject of investigation, out of modesty, fear that the general public would discover their non-maternity, or fear of realizing that the subject was actually too sensitive by opening Pandora's box, Nathalie Rheims accepted my request quickly and simply.

"I don't see why I would hide the reasons why I didn't have a child, today I'm 50, it's too late anyway, and I'm fine with that. I have absolutely no regrets."

For her, not having a baby has been a totally assumed act for a very long time. "I never wanted to have children," she says.

"It goes back to a trauma I had when I was 8 years old, I still remember it very well now. I was raised in a family where books were very important. By the time I was 8 years old, I already loved to read. It was a solitary and endless activity. I often went to my parents' and my father's library. One day, I discovered a medical encyclopedia and plunged into it with an interest that is surely uncommon for a little girl of my age. I came across a drawing of a corpse. The article detailed clinically and scientifically what it meant to die, the stopping of organs, the rotting of the body, the skin, the fact that hair and nails continue to grow, etc. I suddenly became aware of what it meant to die. I was not frightened like an 8 year old girl might be, having nightmares the following nights, but I had an immediate and global understanding of what death meant. For me, for my parents, for everyone I loved. I understood that the death of my loved ones was inevitable, and that made me infinitely sad. Whether we believe in God or not, it is the fate of all of us to return to the earth, to disappear, it is the fate of all of us to have our bodies eaten by worms and reduced to dust. There is nothing we can do about it. Since that day, death has become a familiar subject to me. I have become very interested in it, my universe is impregnated with it.

But how did this enlightened, scientific and lucid conception of death prevent her from becoming a mother?

"The death of all of us is written from the moment we are born, so in my eyes, to give life is to give death. I cannot conceive of bringing a child into the world, because it is to condemn it from its first hours of life. It is illogical and too painful for me. To me, giving birth to a baby would be like

When philosophical convictions take precedence

automatically condemning it to death. I cannot and will not be his executioner."

How did she live this singular conception during her life? Did she have no regrets or hesitations?

"Coincidentally or not, I happened to live with and love men who didn't want children, either because they didn't want to be fathers, or because they already were. However, if I am to be honest to the end, since I told you I would tell you all about it, I had an accident. I was married for years to a man for whom this was not an issue. We were in agreement. And then one day, despite our precautions, I realized that I was pregnant. In this case, what to do? My philosophy has always been to never be the cause of a "murder". I had never wanted to be a mother in order not to be responsible for a future death, so if I was logical with myself, I could not abort. I would have killed an embryo, thus preventing life! I therefore decided to keep the child. My husband followed my decision. Then it turned out that my pregnancy was at risk. I lay down for a while and finally lost my baby. It was almost very serious for my own health, it was very trying."

One can see in this the hand of fate or the confirmation that Nathalie Rheims was not to be a mother. In any case, she did not intervene in this event. Today, she nevertheless has around her subsidiary representations "Claude [Berri] had two sons that I consider my own. I adore them and get along with them very well."

It is also interesting to see - beyond the question of death - that the subject has not disappeared from her interests. Her

No Children. It Makes Sense!

latest film, *Trésor*, is a humorous tale of a couple in their forties who adopt a dog to fill a void. Nathalie, played by Mathilde Seigner, appears very dependent on her emotional desire. Her visceral need to protect a weak being not being satisfied, she literally smothers her husband who obviously does not need to be mothered, and thus offered her an English bull-dog with the sweet name of "Treasure" to keep her busy!

The film constantly evokes, without naming it, the question of a child: to have one or not and for what reason? Nathalie Rheims thus translates into film several questions that many couples ask themselves: beyond their love, what will they build? What will they offer each other? Is there room for a third or fourth person in their home? Are they able to live with someone who interferes with them? How can they make room in their relationship for a child?

Chapter 9

(Pro)Create differently

It is not insignificant to note that among the "childless", there are many artists as well as many executives or people belonging to intellectual professions. Is this a way of saying that we can be fulfilled in other ways? Are creation and procreation twin sisters or antagonistic enemies? Does feminism require motherhood or non-motherhood?

"A thing of intellectuals"?

Is it a coincidence? I have met many women from all walks of life who do not want to become mothers. Among them, many belong to health or related professions (doctors, biologists, psychologists, social workers, etc.). I have therefore chosen to focus here on two of them who, each in their own way, represent the others well. In their impulses, their life environment, their extra-professional activities and their reflections.

Isabelle went to medical school, but she could also have enrolled in a faculty of literature or gone into philosophy. In addition to her work, which is extremely time consuming, she devours books: French and foreign literature, historical and philosophical essays, everything interests her. She lives in Marseille, but doesn't hesitate to take a TGV to go to an exhibition in Paris and to visit friends. In addition to her readings, she is eager to debate, to question the problems of society and the great metaphysical enigmas. My subject of investigation interested her not only because she was involved as a witness, but also because she has always been interested in these questions concerning life. "Not having children? That's an intellectual thing," she said, half amused and half serious. Not exactly a joke...

"I think that in general, intellectuals have fewer children, because they ask themselves the question too much. Coldly, all these considerations lead to the same answer: 'never!' I may have put too much perfection into the notion of parents. The answer to the question 'to have children or not to have children' depends a lot on how high you set the bar, how high you set the role of parenting."

It is obvious that for her, the bar was set high. Too high to ever allow her to answer "yes" to the question that society has asked for her many times.

"When you're in love, you can have an impulse that explains the desire for a child. Personally, I have never felt that way, I have never felt concerned by this reasoning. It is also a question of time, she adds, I was 20 years old in 1977. The seventies were a blessed period, a total explosion of freedom! AIDS did not exist, it was the reign of free love, we benefited from this wave of idyllic freedom. We had, we women, the possibility to completely direct our lives!"

With a degree in psychology, Vanessa has a university diploma in public health and teaches part-time in a nursing school. She is also a regional councillor for the Rhône-Alpes region and a member of the national council of the Socialist Party. "This is my second mandate, I was elected in 1998, until 2011. After that I will stop", she says. For the past thirty years, she has been living in a couple with Nicole, also a local elected official, and deputy principal of an elementary school. At almost 60 years of age, they both never wanted to have children and do not regret it. Their homosexuality? "That's not the reason, if we had wanted to satisfy a desire for motherhood, all we had to do was go abroad!" she says.

In this case, what is at the root of their refusal to become mothers? Rather their lifestyle, their job and their multiple activities and implications.

"I was never interested in motherhood," she says. "Otherwise, I would have gone abroad to be inseminated or to obtain a sperm donation, since at the time, it was still forbidden in France. Some friends had suggested it to me, but

I didn't feel the need. Is it an unconscious censorship? No, I don't think so! I have no problem with this subject, nor with the fact that I live with a woman. I wouldn't have minded raising a child with a woman. The reason is more intimate: I didn't want to."

What was her family's reaction to her life choices? Which of her homosexuality or her refusal of motherhood was less accepted?

"My parents are Catholics, but they have always raised us to be open-minded. They were tolerant of my sexual orientation. However, when I was a young girl, we didn't talk about sexuality, it was the very beginning of the pill, it was still taboo, I didn't know what homosexuality was either. When I met Nicole, I told my parents. Their first question was in relation to motherhood, they immediately made the connection between the two: 'So you won't have a child?' I told them right away that no, I wouldn't have one, not because the law forbade us, but because I didn't want one. I was clear from the beginning."

The reactions in the PS are quite amusing and symptomatic: if people don't pay much attention to their homosexuality, their non-desire to be mothers is questionable:

"In the national council of the Socialist Party, everyone knows that I am gay, I assume totally. When people ask me, 'But you don't have children?' I simply answer them yes."

This does not prevent him from fighting every day for the parents by trying to improve their daily life.

"As an elected official, I do very concrete work. We are in a rural area, we live quite far from major infrastructures, so

No Children. It Makes Sense!

we have few facilities. I fight for the construction of daycare centers, for example. In a way, I feel like I am serving the common good. It requires a lot of investment. Besides, I could never have had the life I have with a child. For me, the issue of the child is the distribution of social roles. Who does the housework in the couple? Who goes to parent-teacher meetings in the evening? In general, women are much more involved. I also intervene for an association of gays and lesbians, many of whom are parents; there are about a hundred couples. This question of the child in the homosexuals challenges me a lot! In our association, there are more women, a certain number of them went to Belgium for artificial inseminations. I'm not against it, but I wonder about this race to have a child that I find in the homosexual community as well as in the heterosexual community. Maybe I'm old-fashioned, but this race at all costs is not my thing. Some children find themselves in ubiquitous situations, parents who hate each other, who do not take care of them. I sincerely believe that in order to blossom, you need love and a structured life. You have to know how to say no to your child, to set limits, not to fall into the trap of the child king. School failure is often rooted in emotional poverty, because parents lose interest in their child. I have the impression, as Coluche used to say, that some people, not all of them of course, have children because they can't have dogs! Nevertheless, I am not against adoption among gay couples. American studies have shown that there are no more homosexuals in homosexual families than in heterosexual families. Even so, our society is not very tolerant overall."

(Pro)Create differently

Artists: creating rather than procreating?

Etymologically, "procreate" is similar to the verb "to create". A simple prefix differentiates them, of Greek origin, which means "for", "in favor of", while they have common synonyms: to give birth, for example. Used literally, it means "to procreate", used figuratively, it means "to create". For the latter, we also have: to imagine, to arrange, to build, to cause, to compose, to conceive, to trigger, to establish, to found, to innovate... The list is long, it shows how much this word is rich in meanings, in variants, in interpretations. To procreate, we have: to give birth, to give life, but also to produce, to proliferate, to multiply, to reproduce. A less dense list, but with multiple nuances. The most tendentious, "to generate", is used in one of the most important prayers of Catholicism, the *Creed*:

I believe in one Lord, Jesus Christ, the only-begotten Son of God, begotten of the Father before all ages; God of God, Light of Light, true God of true God; begotten, not made; of one substance with the Father, by whom all things were made. [...].

To say of Jesus Christ that he is begotten, not created, means that he is the creator and not a creature. This is not the case with children: even when we consider that they are begotten, they do not have the rank of "creators."

Is procreation a creation *ex nihilo* in the same way as artistic creation? Plato, in *The Banquet*, affirms that procreation is creation for dummies, the means for people without talent to ensure themselves an immortal existence in the world. Is the birth of a child reducible to the explosion of an *ego*, are all parents potential narcissists? No, says Jeanne Burgart Goutal in an article entitled *In the name of egotism?*[60]:

"The parents of the future child cannot foresee or program its characteristics: childbirth is therefore an apprenticeship of the loss of mastery, and not an expression of power of the *ego*. [...] There is in the relationship to the child a consensual alienation, a forgetting and giving of oneself."

The pianist, the violinist, the virtuoso flautist, accept as much to alienate themselves for their art, by a way of life which ostracises them from the rest of the mortals. *Ditto* for the writer who doesn't always know where a novel will take him. Like the child to come, the work in progress escapes its author and follows its own path. The writer Amélie Nothomb, a true "writing machine", who publishes one book a year, but writes twice or even three times as many, considers her books as her children and refuses to rework them, because she says "it would be like having an abortion" or asking the surgeon to operate on a child at birth to change the characteristics that do not please. According to her, successful or not, beautiful or not, she must assume her "child".

I find Jane, who refuses that I call her "Madam"; yet she is exactly twenty-nine years older than me. I could be her

---

60. Burgart Goutal (Jeanne), "Au nom de l'égoïsme?", in *Philosophie Magazine*, n° 27, March 2009.

(Pro)Create differently

daughter and it is she who will confide in me in an almost filial movement, or as to an older sister, a friend that I am not.

When I begin my interview, one thing strikes me immediately. Jane is happy, she doesn't pretend, even though she hadn't foreseen that her life would be written without children. In a way, she illustrates a rarer trajectory: how to go from *childless* to *childfree*? Thus, our conversation begins under a new clarity for me. Here is a woman who enjoys the benefits of childlessness without bitterness, without sadness, while having always thought she would have children. How does one go from the certainty of becoming a mother one day to its exact opposite? From the possible joy of giving birth and giving life to the relief of not having been able to do so? Here, it is not a question of confession, but of evidence.

"My husband and I were not medically compatible," she said with a slight shrug. Jane met her husband later than most of her friends.

"I was 39, we got married a year later and immediately tried to have a child. Unsuccessfully."

For more than eighteen months, she agrees to follow the path of the fighter: visits to the gynecologist, medical tests to find out who in the couple is sterile. The problem is complicated, because it turns out that neither of them is completely infertile, the obstacle lies elsewhere. At 40, the human body is slower, less reactive, the doctor's verdict is painful to hear for lovers: "Together, it was impossible. Our equation was wrong medically speaking, while we had no doubt about our love!" After IVF and other assisted reproductive procedures and especially medicated, Jane chooses to stop this vain hunt.

"It's true that I deeply wanted to have a child, but not having one didn't create any drama. You have to face the fact that if nature had not given me this possibility, I had to accept it."

Thus, to hear her tell it, it would be easy to have a zen attitude in front of what many women consider as totally unfair. Is the acceptance of her life, whatever the path, and of a destiny that she would have wished to be different, and moreover different from the one of the majority of women, so easy? Without clashes or personal fracture? How did she operate this translation, this transformation of herself? Does she have a firmer and more joyful character than the other women I have met who seem to have suffered more from the impossibility of giving birth?

"I'm a natural optimist," she confirms to me, "but I think that if I had experienced this ten years earlier, I certainly wouldn't have reacted the same way."

Immediately, I think of the couple's crucial question, sneaky, awful as it is, but so inevitable: what if with another person it could have worked? Did Jane think about doing an artificial insemination with another donor than her husband, or did she think about leaving her husband? The question never crossed her mind.

"A friend of mine asked me if I had considered it to put all my chances on my side. The question caught my attention because I had never thought about it! I had simply presented

(Pro)Create differently

myself with a fait accompli: it wasn't working. At 29, I might have been tempted to persevere in my quest for a child, insisting on treatments that could help fertilization. But by then, I was already old.

Born in 1949 into a family with bourgeois codes reinterpreted in a very free way, Jane grew up in an environment open to the world.

"My mother had us very late, especially for a woman of her time, she was 39 when she gave birth to my older sister and 42 for me. She once wrote, 'I don't want a husband, I want a progenitor.' Extremely unconventional and modern! In the end, she married my father in order to please her parents who found this situation horribly embarrassing."

Influenced by her mother more deeply than she would like to admit, Jane has retained a love of life in all its complexity and all that it has to offer. Thus, in the education she received, there is a certainty that having a child cannot be the sum of her personal growth. Later, Jane would learn from a friend that her mother wondered why she didn't make a baby on her own. This question, too, was quickly put to rest by Jane:

"I didn't feel strong enough. Taking on a child entirely on my own was not for me. I never considered it."

Laurene is younger than Jane. We have already met her a little earlier in this book[61]. She lives and was raised in Paris,

---

61. See Chapter 5.

No Children. It Makes Sense!

in a culturally and socially privileged environment. Laurène locates the birth of her creativity in her childhood.

"I'm an only child, and my mother gave me a very fantasy-based education. We used to play together, she used to tell me a lot of stories. I owe her my artistic sensitivity and the profession I practice today. She herself had a very rigid education. She suffered enormously from it, I believe. Did she want to detach herself from it at all costs? Did I want to detach myself from it? I don't know! I am in a permanent creative process, and there is something alive in creation. This may explain why I have never felt the desire to give birth. Naturally, this must be present in all women. This desire to create, to set up a business, or to produce in one way or another, a being or something else finally, to bring something out of oneself! For the majority of women, perhaps having a child is an affirmation of their creativity, but also a reason to live. I only once had the desire to have a child, with a particular man. I even had a dream, but it was never an obsession. I was pregnant, and then it became an artistic project. So in my dream, I know for sure that I am five months pregnant, yet I have a flat stomach. That's my secret. You can't see it, no one can guess it. This dream seemed to me to be revealing. I wanted to think about its meaning: if I had a child with a man I loved, it would be a matter of chemistry, an alchemy! Of course, I was in love, but just as there are different types of friendship, there are different types of love. It was the first time it happened to me. And then nothing. The thought did cross my mind, but I never thought about it again in terms of desire. I don't usually go after children, some of my friends have them, but I don't want to hold them or keep them.

Laurène offers me her memories in the disorder, she tells her dreams, her childhood:

"Another image that comes to mind is one of smothering: one of my aunts had a child very late in life that she overprotected. On the contrary, I really appreciate the fact that my parents let me become emancipated quickly, I could travel alone even when I was a young teenager. I remember a flight from Paris to Los Angeles. People were almost shocked that I was allowed to make that long trip alone. We agree, every child has his or her own personal sensitivities, inhibitions, and fears (but some parents put their own fears on their children and unconsciously prevent them from acting on them by passing them on). Maybe my parents thought I was capable of being on my own, that I was independent, and if they hadn't thought I was capable, they wouldn't have let me go."

Do we only produce matter and value by making children? Do we not also produce by building, assembling and training people?

I think of Sonia who took over the family workshop at the age of 25, after her father's death. She had been looking for a way, she found it through her father's business, or rather it imposed itself on her in an abrupt and unequivocal way... to the point of filling her whole life.

"It was as if I was pregnant, I took care of it for ten years, it was my own baby. Then, entirely dedicated to her,

No Children. It Makes Sense!

I "nonnized" myself, that is to say, I lived as a bachelor! I went to my friends' weddings, as they went along, all of them got involved and created families while I consolidated my business."

I remember her words when she decided in 2007 to part with the studio by selling it. "It was like a birth or a rescue: my child was out of the water, safe and sound. I could let go of her hand."

The analogy between the company and the child comes from her, not from me. The metaphor is expressive and meaningful enough that I won't dwell on it.

"Being a mother is not giving birth"

Since I am nearing the end of this book, the time has come to add the testimony of a woman, not exactly in the target of those I was looking for at the beginning, and who nevertheless found the right words to evoke this notion of parenthood without having gone through childbirth.

Beatrice is in her fifties and works as a pharmacist in a medium-sized provincial town. Divorced from her first husband with whom she had no children (despite a pregnancy that tragically ended in a therapeutic abortion during which a tube had to be removed), Beatrice remarried at the age of 32 to a man who already had a child. For a very long time, she longed to have a child herself. Life did not give her this opportunity: she became sterile due to an infection.

If I include her here, even though she does not belong to the group of women and men who are the main subject of this book, i.e. those who have not wanted a child, it is because this *childless woman* was able to transform her disillusionment and her "failure" (I ostensibly and voluntarily put this word in quotation marks, because it is understood that it is obviously not a failure in the strict sense of the word, but rather that Beatrice has unfortunately felt her infertility as such for a long time), into a positive adventure, like Jane. How to be happy in spite of an imposed situation? In her case, two elements came to soften her disillusionment: a common passion with her husband, horse riding, and the adoption of a child, born from her husband's first bed.

"With Antoine, we own horses that we have raised. When I met him, I was not riding, while he loved riding. I started riding to please him, and then I got into it completely, until I reached a very good level. Thus, we share a real passion. Taking care of horses requires a daily involvement, a constant attention, like children. That's what being a mother is all about, knowing how to take care of others, giving your time, and not giving birth. In my eyes, finally, giving birth is not the criterion that defines the word *mother*. Being a mother, like being a father, is a question of transmitting knowledge, culture; passing on messages, I wanted to be a good coach to my adopted son."

Now appeased, she prefers not to choose "her side" and advocates tolerance towards those who are not tempted by parenthood.

"Parents are scouts and leaders. However, I don't think I'm any better than anyone else; everyone does as they please, as they can. To have a child or not is a personal choice, to have a great career or not. We must leave the choice to young women, we must not force them, put pressure on them one way or the other. The most important thing is to have the possibility to choose. When people are influenced from the outside, they are led down a path that is not their own. Deciding to have a child means planning for the aftermath, and therefore assuming responsibility. But if you don't want to, you shouldn't be ashamed. On the other hand, you only live once. You have to think about it carefully."

Conclusion

"Find your way, be in tune with yourself"

As I close this book, I would like to leave aside the arguments of the various parties and focus on the outcome. To have or not to have a child: the common point between those who say yes and those who say no is the quest for personal well-being. As Laurène told me, "the most important thing is to know what your path is, that's happiness".

What couple has never found itself faced with the alternative? In the end, it doesn't matter what the answer is when the question is approached honestly, head-on, and with true intellectual generosity. It is crucial that each person in the couple, the woman and the man, or the two men and the two women if it is a homosexual couple, can give their opinion, share with the other their possible fears and doubts. It is essential to show empathy towards each other. In order for the listening to be real, two conditions must be met: knowing how to hear and knowing how to say. When the unsaid things proliferate, when the knots are passed under silence, retracted or truncated, they risk to tighten and to cause deep blockings, auguring great sufferings.

Hervé avoids talking about it with his friend. He knows that she doesn't take such a strict or irrevocable line as his: "She doesn't say, 'I don't want to have them,' she says, 'This is not the time.' We don't talk about it often, only when she sees pictures of her nieces and nephews. I think that if she really wants one, she will have to leave me, it's too important a subject for either of us to make a definitive concession to the other. The child as a cement of the couple, there is nothing worse for me. I don't approve of those who do it to try to mend fences. It's doomed to failure."

During my investigation, I also tried to find out if parents and non-parents were like cats and dogs. Among the *no-kids,* two camps can be distinguished: those who live their choice gently and the angry ones who claim their difference and demand that the majority give them more say and show more tolerance towards them. If Frédérique Longrée and Théophile de Giraud belong to the angry ones, Joshua and Stanislas, although very extreme in their positions (the latter would like to undergo a vasectomy), refuse to be labeled or framed: "I don't want to ghettoize myself by joining anti-natalist groups," Joshua confided to me. "It's a private, personal choice." Stanislas also does not want to "join a group like the *no-kids*: it's not for me! I don't like to belong to a caste or a sect. Everyone is free to think and live as they wish as long as they do not harm others."

It's one thing to say it, but the reality of the situation is sometimes different. Non-parents spend more time with each other: "I have a lot of female friends and acquaintances around me who don't have children," says Suzanne. "Some are single, like me, others are married."

What is the reason for this form of endogamy? Is it because they feel rejected? While I have met women who have suffered from their singularity, Suzanne has softened this image by confiding to me that she has not been stigmatized: "Men have never reproached me for not wanting a child. It was simply never discussed with them. It has not been a source of dispute or rejection in my life."

For her part, she notes with relief that "the image of the childless woman has evolved. People don't ask me that question anymore. Even my mother agrees with me, she often tells me: 'I'm happy to see you like this, fulfilled, balanced and happy'. I have the impression that the subject has become commonplace in France." However, she admits that "it depends on the social environment. I evolve in a circle of people for whom freedom is fundamental."

So if they don't feel singled out, what's driving childless women to see each other more frequently? "The main reason? They have free time." Even Joshua, who argued earlier for a mix of groups, admits that while he hangs out with "parents as well as couples and singles without children," he "prefers to spend evenings with people who didn't bring their kids with them! I want to remain flexible and tolerant. On the other hand, it would bother me to spend entire vacations with children around me: we don't do the same things, the rhythm is not the same."

In addition, it is clear that, outside of the interviews I used for my survey, the "non-parents" hardly talk about children! It is normal that if they don't want them, they are not at the center of their concerns. The issue is rarely discussed, either with friends or family. "Yes, I've definitely talked about it once or twice, but it's not something that's on my mind. I never think about it," says Hervé. "If I discuss it, it's because someone has asked me, for example my mother. She often asks me if she will be a grandmother one day." A way to ward off possible pressure? "No, because nobody can put it on me, not my mother, not my friends, not my girlfriend. I don't want it and the others won't change my mind. Their point of view is not mine. That's it."

In light of what they said, whatever the difficulty of assuming their choice at the time, my participants have in common that they have no regrets; on the contrary, they feel strengthened over the years in their decision. Sonia says that "not having had a child is not at all a wound or a crack". On the other hand, she considers that "if [she] had not known True Love, it would have been terrible." Suzanne believes that children, like marriage, "are not an end in themselves. I believe in the circumstances of life. It didn't happen for me, you should never regret the paths you take. The same goes for Vanessa: "Not having a child does not weigh on me, even with time, I have never regretted this choice. To tell the truth, I don't ask myself the question! I never say to myself 'I missed my life!'" She adds that her partner didn't question it either. "We lived in the middle of the post-Sixties era. She had a straight life before she met me and I knew she had performed an abortion. With her, the desire for a child did not exist. At no time did we hesitate."

Recently, a meeting reinforced Suzanne's decision not to have a child. Thanks to the social networks that flourish on the Internet, she met a former lover.

"After twenty-eight years of silence, I found on the Web my Great Love, we had met in England when I was a young au pair. We started a letter exchange: he had married and then divorced, and was the father of two grown-up children. He wanted to see me again, I was anxious, but I said to myself 'why not'. The shock was terrible, because I was extremely disappointed! He looked even more beaten than down, and had completely lost the aura I had known him for at the time of our romance. He, on the other hand, was full of admiration for me, especially for my choice. He told me that I had always known how to direct my life and that he had been subjected to it. He regretted having had children, getting married and getting involved."

This book is now finished. I modestly tried to show that another way was possible outside of parenthood, that

"Find your way, be in tune with yourself"

non-parents were as fulfilled and interesting as the others, and, although they were in the minority, that they were not on the margins of society, but were fully participating in its evolution. Let's hope that in the future, this difference will no longer be considered as a defect or as a lack.

I would like to add a word specifically about women: from time immemorial, they have been considered as potential mothers. In his essay, *Les Structures élémentaires de la parenté*, Claude Lévi-Strauss points out that in all societies, "the bond of reciprocity which founds marriage is not established between men and women, but between men by means of women who are only the principal occasion for it. [...] Matrilineal filiation is the hand of the father or the brother of the woman which extends to the village of the brother." The woman exists for what she represents, not for what she is.

Therefore, refusing to be a mother, and still living in the light, is an eminently feminist act in itself. Even when it is not thought of as such. In the fact of refusing to have children, lies also the idea of non-alignment: not to do like everyone else, by refusing the dimension and the animal domination in one's life. In view of the centuries that preceded us, centuries that forged and imposed a predominantly male mentality, it is also undeniably a courageous and anti-conformist act.

Not having children is the choice of those I interviewed. And what is yours? What does your little voice tell you? How is your inner child doing?

In conclusion, know how to listen to yourself, not lie to yourself and resist the ambient diktat. To say "I will not have children" is to accept to be different, to have a destiny that differs from that of the majority. This is not an easy path for everyone. To be in agreement with your own model, while being part of the minority... and to be happy in this way.

Lexicon

Nullipare: Adjective and feminine singular noun of the 19th century, composed from Latin *nullus* ("none") and *parere* ("to give birth"). Refers to a woman who has never borne a child or who has not yet given birth to a child; characterizes a female mammal before her first gestation, a female mosquito before its first laying. In medicine: who has never given birth (Antonym: parturient).

Primigeste: pregnant woman for the first time.

Multigeste: woman who has had several pregnancies.

Multipare: woman who has had two or more births.

The Pill:
Behind this discovery, a man! Gregory Goodwin Pincus, American physician and biologist, who died in 1967. It is

funny to think that one of the greatest tools for women's liberation was thought up and developed by a man. However, the story would not be complete if I did not mention Katherine McCormick, who devoted her fortune to this research, and Margaret Sanger, a New York nurse and founder of family planning. By the way, what is a pill? The first one, called Enovid, is the result of a combination of progesterone and synthetic estrogen. We owe the very first discoveries at the hormonal level to the Austrian doctor Haberlandt who obtained positive results on animals. The principle will be the same for women: it is a question of delaying ovulation by injection of estrogen. The first tests did not succeed in completely blocking ovulation, only constraining the regulation of the menstrual cycle. About ten years later, further research on synthetic hormones led to the discovery that it was possible to block the ovulation process by stimulating the activity of these glands with a drug[62].

Marketed for the first time in Germany as early as 1956, then put on sale in the United States one year later, the pill is mainly used by doctors to treat disorders in certain patients. In 1960, it was used as a full-fledged contraceptive. As the pill entered the world market, the most conservative governments were opposed to it. The battle for fertility control was on. Around 1965, 5 million American women were using it; in France, the pill was legally distributed in pharmacies from 1967. Its diffusion first affected the

---

62. *In* RÉGNIER-LOILIER (Arnaud), *Avoir des enfants en France, désirs et réalités,* éditions de l'Ined, 2007.

No Children. It Makes Sense!

youngest, most urbanized and most educated segment of the population, before spreading to all social backgrounds, age groups and regions[63].

With the pill, the dissociation desired and expected by many women between the sexual act on the one hand, and procreation on the other, is finally possible. Their wish is granted. Two conditions underlie this new reality: legislation in line with these scientific discoveries (this is still not the case in many countries) and the next logical step: the legalization of abortion. Women who want to control their births and who take the pill or use other contraceptive methods such as the IUD, spermicidal creams, condoms, and the diaphragm, also want to be able to remedy unwanted fertilization. The debate rages on, more so than for the pill. In 1971, *Le Nouvel Observateur* kicked off the debate and publicized the problem by publishing the "Manifesto of the 343", which brought together women, both famous and unknown, who had had recourse to abortion in their lives (voluntary interruption of pregnancy). The scandal at the time was also about the hypocrisy surrounding abortions, which were performed in sordid conditions, abroad or at home, in the homes of angel makers, in full illegality. In January 1975, the Veil law was adopted by 284 votes to 189. The Vatican expressed its strong opposition, but so did groups of doctors who spoke of racial eugenics. Today, abortion plays a very important role in birth control, since in metropolitan France (according to a study

---

63. *Ibid.*

by Vilain in 2005), 203,346 abortions were performed in 2003, for 761,464 births.

More generally, contraceptive methods have helped to reduce unwanted births significantly, the direct consequence of which was a decline in fertility around 1965. From 1963-1967 to 1983-1987, the proportion of unwanted births fell from 1 in 5 to 1 in 10[64].

64. Study by Henri Leridon and Laurent Toulemon, *in* "Démographie : approche statistique et dynamique des populations", Economica, 1997.

Table of contents

Best sellers Max Milo Editions

Hitler's banker, Jean-François Bouchard

Confessions of a forger, Éric Piedoie Le Tiec

The Koran and the flesh, Ludovic-Mohamed Zahed

Governing by fake news, Jacques Baud

Governing by chaos, Collectif

A political history of food, Paul Ariès

Mad in U.S.A.: The ravages of the "American model",
Michel Desmurget

Mondial soccer club geopolitics, Kévin Veyssière

Putin: Game master?, Jacques Braud

Treatise on the three impostors: Moses, Jesus, Muhammad,
The Spirit of Spinoza

TV Lobotomy, Michel Desmurget